CROSS ✦ ROADS

Jesus IN THE *New Testament*

Author
Richard J. Reichert

BROWN-ROA

A Division of Harcourt Brace & Company

BROWN-ROA
A Division of Harcourt Brace & Company

O u r   M i s s i o n

The primary mission of BROWN-ROA is to provide the
Catholic and Christian educational markets with the
highest quality catechetical print and media resources.
The content of these resources reflects the best insights
of current theology, methodology, and pedagogical research.
The resources are practical and easy to use, designed to meet
expressed market needs, and written to reflect the
teachings of the Catholic Church.

Nihil Obstat

Rev. Richard L. Schaefer

Imprimatur

✠ Most Rev. Jerome Hanus, O.S.B.

Archbishop of Dubuque

January 4, 1998

Feast of Saint Elizabeth Ann Seton

The Imprimatur is an official declaration that a book or pamphlet is free of doctrinal or moral
error. No implication is contained therein that anyone who granted the Imprimatur agrees with
the contents, opinions, or statements expressed.

Illustrations: Rob Suggs

Photo Credits: Gene Plaisted, OSC/THE CROSIERS—4, 7, 8, 14, 34, 36, 58, 63, 68, 70, 71, 77, 80, 90,
102, 106; James L. Shaffer—6, 19, 20, 28T, 39, 42L, 49, 55, 82, 88, 104; Skjold Photography—22, 47;
Jim Whitmer—28L, 28R, 42R, 43L, 43R, 85, 92, 94

Printed in the United States of America.

ISBN 0-15-950471-6

Coming Attractions

Introduction

A fresh look...

Dear young person,

You've probably been hearing about Jesus and the stories about him in the New Testament for as long as you can remember. As you begin another course about him, you may be asking, "Is this really necessary? Won't it be boring to cover the same old stuff again?"

To get the right slant on things before you begin this course, here are a few ideas to consider:

- Up to now, much of what you've learned about Jesus you've been hearing "with a child's ears" and thinking about "with a child's mind." But you are no longer a child. You're quickly leaving childhood behind, and you've been acquiring a more adult way of thinking the last year or so.

- It's time to set aside many of your childhood ideas about Jesus and take a fresh look at who he really is. It's time to put all the little pieces together and form a clear, more organized view of Jesus' life, what he has meant for the world, and what he means for you.

- If you take this course seriously, you can become something of an "expert" on who you are, who Jesus is, and what his life means to you.

So we invite you to approach this course with an open mind. If you can do this, you'll be able to answer Jesus' question, "Who do you say that I am?" in an entirely new way. You'll also discover a lot about yourself and about your growing faith.

Richard Reichert

Green Bay, Wisconsin

? ?? Who am I? ?? ?

How do we really know who another person is? Play this game to find out.

For each person in the group, you'll need:

- paper or 3 X 5 card,
- marker or pen
- straight pin

Directions

1. Distribute the paper, markers, and pins to everyone.
2. Think of a famous person (athlete, movie or TV star, political figure, and so on) who is living or dead. Secretly write that person's name on the paper.
3. Pin the paper to the back of another student's shirt or sweater.
4. Find out whose name is on your back by asking questions of other students.

Rule: They can only give you clues! They can't tell you the person's name.

Keep asking questions until you find out who you are.

? ?? Who are you? ?? ?

In this space, write down some "clues" that will help others get to know who you are right now.

My complete name _____

My favorite food _____

My favorite animal _____

My favorite color _____

My favorite TV show _____

My favorite hobby or fun activity _____

Share these clues with one other person. Ask that person to share his or her clues with you. Then take turns introducing one another to the group.

It Doesn't Make Sense

Why Jesus?

In one way, it would make more sense for you to be starting a book about Julius Caesar or Alexander the Great than to be starting one about Jesus the Nazarene. Caesar and Alexander were famous men in their day. They were great generals. They both built world empires and ruled them well. Some of their policies and decisions still have effects on our world today.

Jesus was just the opposite. He was born into a working-class family. As far as we know, he had only a minimum education. He grew up in Nazareth, a small town in Judea, an unimportant country controlled by the Roman Empire. Jesus never traveled more than three hundred miles from the place where he was born. After his foster father died, we assume that Jesus supported himself and his mother by working as a carpenter or general handyman.

When Jesus did "go public" around age thirty, he was a wandering preacher. He never wrote anything or invented anything. He never led an army, conquered any country, or held an official office. He just preached to whomever would listen.

Jesus did manage to gather a small band of faithful disciples who stayed with him and helped him throughout the three years he preached. But even they abandoned him at the end.

Some religious leaders finally arranged to have Jesus arrested one night. They held a quick trial and found him guilty of crimes against the Jewish religion. The next day they pressured the Roman governor, Pilate, into condemning Jesus to be crucified.

Meanwhile, Jesus' closest friends and followers all fled and hid, afraid that they might be arrested and executed, too. Only Jesus' mother, a few other women, and John, one of his disciples, stayed around. They had to borrow a tomb to bury Jesus, for the only property Jesus owned when he died were the clothes on his back. (Actually, Jesus didn't have these, either, because the soldiers who executed him divided them up among themselves.)

So why in the world should we be studying about Jesus the Nazarene today instead of Caesar or Alexander the Great?

What Do You Think?

In the first column, write down facts YOU already know about Jesus. After each fact write down where you learned this information.

Now form small groups, and in the second column, add facts shared by others in your group. This will give you a more complete story about Jesus.

Finally, discuss with your small group why people today should study about Jesus. In the third column, list at least three reasons.

Facts about Jesus	More facts about Jesus	Why study about Jesus?
preach was chirchan Jesus was Jewish Christ Christians were follower of Jesos Chirst	preched when he was 60 John sautayed stayed w/ him	to learn cristinty how to help people

Share your group's reasons with the class. As a class, agree on the three most important reasons people today should study about Jesus. Place an asterisk next to the reason YOU want to study about Jesus.

Looking for Answers!

Check the correct reference.

The tomb in which Jesus was buried belonged to:

_____ a. Matthew 17:9

_____ b. Luke 7:18–19

_____ c. Matthew 27:57–60

_____ d. John 19:30

Answer: _____

It Didn't End There

Jesus' execution and burial were not the end of his story. Rather, they were the beginning of his role in human history.

On the third day after his death, Jesus' followers experienced something that changed their lives. Jesus reappeared to them, alive and transformed! He didn't just come back to life, which would mean that he could suffer and undergo death again. Rather, Jesus was alive in a new way. He literally conquered death.

What do we know about Jesus' new life after death? As the New Testament tells us, time, space, gravity, and the other laws of the physical world had no power over him. Yet he could eat and drink and talk with his disciples. He was the same Jesus the Nazarene, but in a resurrected, transformed state. There was no denying he had been killed. Now, with their own eyes, people saw him alive again.

The followers who experienced Jesus in his resurrected state began to see everything Jesus had taught and everything he had done in a whole new light. It finally became clear to them that this carpenter's son from Nazareth was the Messiah, or Savior, whom God had been promising to send since the beginning of Hebrew history.

I·AM·THE·RESURRECTION·AND·THE·LIFE·

Catechism Clip

Jesus means in Hebrew: "God saves." At the annunciation, the angel Gabriel gave him the name Jesus as his proper name, which expresses both his identity and his mission. [Cf. Lk 1:31]. . . The word "Christ" comes from the Greek translation of the Hebrew Messiah, *which means "anointed." It became the name proper to Jesus only because he accomplished perfectly the divine mission that "Christ" signifies.* (430, 436)

Now the disciples saw Jesus differently. This former carpenter who was executed as a criminal and buried in a borrowed tomb was the Messiah! This preacher whom they had talked with and worked with for three years was, in fact, God's Son. This man whom they saw sweat as he walked along, who enjoyed a good cup of wine, who could laugh with children was God's Anointed, the Conqueror of evil and death. This man—who had sore feet at the end of a long journey, who was as eager as anyone for a drink of cool water in the afternoon heat, who huddled near the fire at night to keep the chill off—was the Son of God!

It seemed impossible. It seemed too good to be true. It didn't make sense, at least in any human terms. But the fact remained: Jesus did conquer death. The disciples saw him, touched him, heard him, and ate with him after his return.

It suddenly became very clear to these eye-witnesses just what they must do. They must proclaim this good news to anyone who would listen: Jesus has come to free us from evil and death. Jesus the Nazarene is the Messiah and the Son of the Living God!

Looking for Answers!

Check the correct reference.
When Simon Peter and the other disciples saw the resurrected Jesus, the activity in which they were involved was:
_____ a. Mark 8:11–13
_____ b. John 21:11–13
_____ c. Luke 21: 29–33
_____ d. John 13:36–38
Answer: _____fishing_____

Life After Death

Share with the group any story you know (from the TV news, a magazine, a personal experience, or the newspaper) about someone who apparently died and then was resuscitated. What happened?

How are the examples of resuscitation different from the resurrection of Jesus?

Scripture Search

Read the following story about the risen Jesus: John 20:24–29. Then answer these questions.

1. Which disciple had not been present when Jesus first appeared to the Twelve?

   Tomas

2. What was this disciple's response to the others' declaration that they had seen the resurrected Jesus?

   happy 3 days 5 days

3. How much time passed before Jesus again appeared to the disciples?

4. What were Jesus' words to the disciple who had doubted his first appearance?

   Blessed are those nol dont need to see to believe

5. Write verse 29 here:

6. When are times in your life that you need proof in order to believe something?

   snow sean

7. When are times in your life that you believe in something, even though you cannot see it?

   plants going around sun

8. What helps you believe in Jesus' love, even though he does not humanly walk on our earth today?

   helps people

9. What would you say to the risen Jesus if he appeared to you today?

   hi

Believe it or not

Not everyone believed the story of Jesus' resurrection when it first took place. The Gospel of Matthew tells us how the Jewish leaders spread rumors that Jesus' followers had simply stolen his body from the tomb and then made up the story of his resurrection. Some people accepted those rumors as truth.

It's been the same throughout history. There have been many attempts to explain away the resurrection. Some people have argued that Jesus never really died on the cross. They say that he merely passed out or went into a coma. When he was placed in the cool tomb and allowed to rest, he recovered and then got out. Some have argued that Jesus never appeared to his followers; instead, they experienced a kind of group hypnosis or group hallucination.

Some nonbelievers have even tried to make Jesus' death and resurrection into a fantastic plot cooked up by Jesus himself. They say that Jesus and the soldiers were in it together. They were to fake Jesus' death so that when he reappeared, Jesus could say he had returned from death and so gain new followers.

Obviously, not everyone was willing to accept the message the apostles preached. But the apostles never gave up. They spoke with such conviction and belief in Jesus' resurrection that two thousand years later Christians still preach the same message: Jesus is risen. Jesus has conquered sin and death. Jesus is Lord! Indeed, history has never been the same since that first Easter morning.

CHECK IT OUT!

The word *Easter* comes from *Eastre*, the name of the Greek goddess of Spring.

🖝 The debate 🖝

Suppose a nonbelieving friend came to you and said one of the following statements. What argument would you use to help your friend be more open to Jesus?

Nonbeliever:

1. Jesus didn't rise from the dead because he never really died. He just faked his death.

2. There's a medical explanation for the resurrection. People thought Jesus was dead because he was in a coma. But later, in the tomb, he woke up.

3. Jesus never appeared after his death to the apostles. They lied so that they could start the Church and become important.

4. Jesus never appeared to the apostles after his death. The apostles were hallucinating.

What I would say:

1. _____
_____
_____

2. _____
_____
_____
_____

3. _____
_____
_____
_____

4. _____
_____
_____

Discuss your arguments with the class. If time permits, form teams and debate one of the four arguments.

The stone of anointing at the Church of the Holy Sepulchre in Jerusalem

Amazing! Incredible!

Against All Odds

When you think of it, the first ones to believe that Jesus is Lord, Messiah, and Son of God did seem to have an impossible task. Imagine yourself going up to a stranger and saying something such as: "I was a follower of this carpenter-turned-preacher for several years. Then the government officials had him executed as a criminal. Three days later he reappeared to us alive, transformed. He's the Savior of the world. So why don't you become his follower, too?"

Chances are, there's no way you'd ever do this. It'd be too embarrassing. People would think you were crazy. But that's exactly what the apostles and other disciples of Jesus began to do. They talked to anyone who would listen. They repeated the same story, announcing the good news that Jesus was Lord and that God's reign had begun. Some people did laugh at the apostles and thought they were crazy. Others, especially some religious leaders, did everything they could to stop them from spreading this "nonsense" about Jesus.

But the amazing thing is this: Many people did believe the apostles and disciples! With God's grace, these people also became followers of Jesus. In turn, they joined the apostles and other disciples in announcing this good news to their own friends and neighbors.

In the first three centuries after Jesus' death, faith in him spread throughout the known world. During those centuries, nonbelievers killed people because they refused to reject their belief that Jesus is the Son of God. It's something of a miracle that faith in Jesus got started at all. It's an even greater wonder that it survived. After all, the strongest government in the world, the Roman Empire, tried to stamp it out. Nevertheless, faith in Jesus survived and spread. The rest is history. Now, two thousand years later, about one-third of all people are Christians, followers of Christ. They accept the good news about Jesus.

CHECK IT OUT!

Christianity became a tolerated religion of the Roman Empire about three hundred years after Jesus died. Today, the Catholic faith is growing faster in Africa than in any other country in the world. Seventy percent of the world's Catholics live below the equator.

Scripture Search

Awe came upon everyone, because many wonders and signs were being done by the apostles. All who believed were together and had all things in common; they would sell their possessions and goods and distribute the proceeds to all, as any had need. Day by day, as they spent much time together in the temple, they broke bread at home and ate their food with glad and generous hearts, praising God and having the goodwill of all the people. And day by day the Lord added to their number those who were being saved. (Acts 2:43–47)

- What is most appealing to you about the lifestyle of the apostles?

- What would you find challenging about such a lifestyle?

Reporting the good news

As a newspaper reporter, you have just been assigned to write an article on what the apostles were preaching about Jesus' life and message. The sources for your information are Peter's words in Acts 2:22–36 and Paul's words in 1 Corinthians 15:1–19. Read these passages and then write a short article about the gospel (good news) that the followers of Jesus proclaimed. Use a separate piece of paper for your rough draft. Then write your final draft here.

Headline: _____

Article: _____

_____

_____

_____

_____

_____

_____

_____

_____

_____

_____

_____

_____

1. What do you think it would take for you to become excited enough and brave enough to risk embarrassment and proclaim the good news about Jesus to others?

_____

_____

2. How do you think you might act if Christians began to be persecuted in your hometown tomorrow?

_____

_____

_____

Looking for Answers!

As followers rooted deeply in our union with Jesus Christ, we are to be strong in the virtue of:

_____ a. Colossians 2:6–7

_____ b. Galatians 3:1–2

_____ c. 2 Corinthians 7:12–13

_____ d. Hebrews 11:29

Answer: _____

Your turn

You never had a chance to meet Jesus the Nazarene firsthand or to see him face-to-face after his resurrection. You believe that he is God's Son because you've taken someone else's word for it.

Whoever told you this good news heard it from someone else. It's a story that's been handed down from generation to generation for almost two thousand years. It's a faith that's been handed down despite millions of efforts to the contrary. A faith so powerful that it can last so long against that kind of opposition must have truth on its side. It certainly can't be taken lightly or called unimportant.

Even though you can consider yourself lucky that you heard this good news and received this faith when you were still young, this can create its own problem. People who have always had faith can tend to take it for granted. It doesn't seem like such a big deal. It's not easy to get excited about it the way the first Christians did.

That's going to be one of the goals of this course—trying to meet Jesus firsthand, the way the first disciples did. Your challenge is to take a fresh look at this good news and see if you can feel some of the same excitement and joy and personal friendship for Jesus that the first Christians experienced. Believe it or not, Jesus had you and me in mind when he told his apostles:

Have you become a believer because you have seen me?

Blessed are those who have not seen and yet have come to believe. (John 20:29)

Jesus knew that someday we new believers would be around. He's been waiting for the chance to help you get to know him better. Now that chance has arrived. You stand at the crossroads. It's your turn to become an adult disciple, a mature believer, a personal friend of Jesus the Nazarene, who is also your Lord.

Reflection

"Go into all the world and proclaim the good news to the whole creation." (Mark 16:15)

Briefly discuss how you can proclaim the good news today.

Here is one way I will share the good news with another person this week:
example

_____

_____

_____

Jesus,

Help me share the good news with my family and friends.

Help me put aside my embarrassment and reluctance to talk about you with others.

Help me be open and sincere in my relationship with you.

Amen.

Homework

Use the following Scripture passages to fill in the blanks:

- John 20:24–29
- Acts 2:22–36
- Luke 24:36–49
- 1 Corinthians 15:1–19

So the other disciples said to Thomas, "We have seen (1) __Jesus__." But Thomas said to them, "Unless I see (2) __holes__ in his hands and put my finger into the nail marks and put my hand into his side, I will (3) __not believe__." . . .Thomas answered and said to Jesus, (4) "__I believe__!" Jesus said to him, "Have you come to believe because you have seen me? Blessed are those who (5) __don't see__ and have believed." . . . "God raised this Jesus, of this we are all (6) __saved witness__. While they were still speaking about this, Jesus stood in their midst and said to them, (7) "__Peace be with you__." . . . Then he opened their minds to understand the (8) _____. And he said to them, "Thus it is written that (9) __Jesus__ would suffer and (10) __rise__ on the third day and that repentance, for the forgiveness of sins, would be (11) _____ in his name to all the nations, beginning in (12) _____. . . . Now I am reminding you of the (13) __gospel__ I preached to you, which you indeed received and in which you also stand. For if the dead are not raised, and if Christ has not been (14) __raised__, your faith is (15) __vain__.

Where You Come From

You are where you grow up

Where you grow up—its geography, its history, its culture, and its politics—has a big influence on you. It influences how you think, what you like, how you act, and even how you dress. In other words, your "environment" affects who you are right now and who you are becoming. Just think about it: How have each of the following influences shaped who you are?

My environment	Influence on me
1. Supper table conversation	1.
2. Neighborhood	2.
3. Friends	3.
4. Older teens you know or see on the street	4.
5. Parents	5.
6. Other relatives or adults	6.
7. School	7.
8. TV	8.
9. Music	9.
10. Town or city	10.

Share your answers in a small group. Then work together to make a list of 5 key ideas you have as a result of these influences.

Key ideas:

1. _____

2. _____

3. _____

4. _____

5. _____

Share these ideas with the class.

Jesus' Environment

Just like you, Jesus was shaped by his local environment—by the supper table talk, by playing with friends, by watching older people on the streets. Thus, to understand who Jesus really is, we have to learn about his "roots." Those roots are Jewish.

The Jewish (Israelite) people are unique in all the world because they were the first people to know God in a relational way. Their belief in a personal God began with Abraham, who lived about 3800 years ago. The Jewish people saw themselves as God's chosen people, a small nation trying to remain faithful to the one, true God. They lived 1800 years amid some of the most powerful empires the world has ever seen—Egyptians, Persians, Babylonians, and Romans. All these empires conquered the Jews at one time or another, and all of them tried to convert the Jews to their beliefs.

This environment greatly affected Jesus. He grew up amid people who had a fierce loyalty to God, whose name was revealed to Moses. When Jesus' family, friends, or neighbors talked about the Law, they meant the Law of Moses and the covenant that the Jews had formed with God 1200 years before. For Jesus and for the Jews of his time, the most important place on earth wasn't Rome, but the Temple at Jerusalem. The Temple was the symbol of God's continuing presence among the Jewish people. It was the most holy place on earth.

CHECK IT OUT!

The Temple was first built by King Solomon (the son of King David) in 950 B.C.E. The Temple was destroyed in 587 B.C.E., rebuilt in 520 B.C.E., and destroyed for good in 70 C.E. Only one wall, the western wall, or Wailing Wall, remains of the last Temple.

King David was the Isrealites' most famous king. He lived about 950 years before Jesus was born. His reign was a golden age for the Israelites, and they loved to recall it. They clung to God's promise to one day send a messiah, a descendant of David, to reestablish a perfect kingdom of peace and justice.

By the time Jesus was growing up in Nazareth, the Jewish people's hope for the messiah was strong. Many talked about it and expected this messiah any day. He would appear, rally the people, drive out the Romans, and reestablish David's kingdom of peace and justice. You can bet Jesus heard the following talk in the streets of Nazareth:

- There is only one God, the God of our father, Abraham.
- We are God's chosen people.
- The covenant is the only Law.
- The Temple is the house of God, and Jerusalem is God's holy city.
- The messiah is coming soon to reestablish the kingdom of David.

Indeed, these were the five key ideas that shaped Jesus as he grew up in Nazareth. They were some of his most important roots.

Street scene in modern Nazareth

Four Jewish VIPs

Form groups of four. Have each person choose one of the following VIPs (Very Important Persons) in Jewish history. Read the Scripture passages about your VIP. Take notes. Then tell the group what you learned.

VIP	Notes
Abraham: Father of the Jewish people; lived about 1800 B.C.E.	
Genesis 12:1–7	
Genesis 17:1–9	
Genesis 22:1–18	
Moses: Responsible for the Law and covenant; lived about 1200 B.C.E.	
Exodus 3:1–10	
Exodus 13:17–22	
Exodus 20:18–22	
David: Israel's most famous king; reigned about 950 B.C.E.	
1 Samuel 17	
2 Samuel 5:1–4	
2 Samuel 7:8–16	
Solomon: David's son	
1 Kings 3:7–14	
1 Kings 6:1	
1 Kings 8:22–26	

If you could be one of these VIPs, who would you be? Why?

The Infancy Narratives

The stories of Jesus' birth and earliest years are called the *infancy narratives*. The Gospels of Matthew and Luke begin with these stories. Each Gospel tells the story from a different angle, giving spearate details of the account. After reading both stories, fill in the chart below as completely as you can. You may have some empty boxes.

	Matthew 1:18–2:11	Luke 2:1–40
Jesus' mother and foster father		
Town and region of birthplace		
Jesus' bed		
Visitors		
Visitors' gifts		
Ruler at the time		
Date of circumcision		
Sacrifice given when Jesus is presented in the Temple		
Town and region of new hometown		

Where in the world is Nazareth?

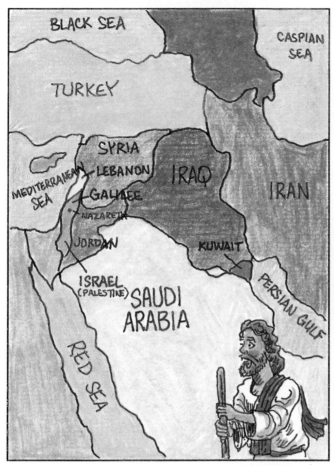

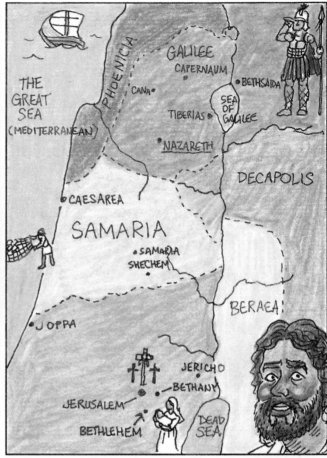

Nazareth was in Galilee, the northern part of Palestine. Galilee, a mixture of hills and fertile plains, was ideal for farming and for raising sheep. Jesus learned about farming and shepherding when he was growing up by watching the life around him.

One special feature of Galilee was its fresh-water lake, the Sea of Galilee. It was full of fish. Thus many of the people in the towns around Nazareth were involved in fishing. Jesus grew up loving that lake. He learned a lot about fishing. Chances are he learned to swim in those blue waters. So Jesus grew up surrounded by simple, hard-working folk—farmers, shepherds, and fishermen.

But Jesus also had a good view of the bigger world because Galilee was right on a major trade route. Caravans of merchants from faraway lands came through regularly. They'd come from as far as Rome in the west and India in the east. They'd come from Egypt in the south and Syria in the north. Roman regiments marched by. Jesus probably saw people from every nation and race at some time or other as he was growing up. Even if it was just in passing, he heard many languages, saw unusual clothes, caught glimpses of exotic animals, and heard snatches of news from all parts of the world. All these experiences shaped him.

CHECK IT OUT!

The Sea of Galilee is about seven miles long and three and a half miles wide.

Jesus performed many miracles in the towns of the region of Galilee. Read about the following miracles. Write down where each miracle occurred and a brief summary of the miracle itself.

Mark 2:1–5

Location:

Summary:

Luke 7:1–10

Location:

Summary:

Luke 4:31–37

Location:

Summary:

John 2:1–11

Location:

Summary:

Now read Mark 6:1–6. Why is it that very few people were healed in Jesus' hometown of Nazareth in Galilee?

Day-to-day life in Nazareth

In Jesus' time, the most common food of people who were poor was a coarse bread made from barley. (Only people who were wealthy could afford bread made from wheat.) Such bread was a rare treat for the poor. Honey, not sugar, was used to sweeten food. There weren't many cows, so milk came mostly from sheep and goats.

Eating meat or eggs was a luxury few people could afford, except on a special occasion. But fish, a good source of protein, was fairly plentiful and inexpensive. Fish were most often dried or smoked. Fresh fish was available only near the shores where it was caught, because the hot climate made it spoil quickly. Vegetables such as lentils, cucumbers, onions, and lettuce were plentiful, as were fruits and nuts, such as, grapes, dates, olives, figs, melons, apricots, pomegranates, walnuts, almonds, and pistachios.

Most people prepared food over open fires, and some people used clay ovens. In places like Jerusalem, smoke from cooking fires got so thick that open fires were outlawed. Wood could be hard to find and expensive. Water was also precious in many areas of the country, especially during the dry season. Wells played an important part in the social life of the women, who had to gather there each day to get the day's supply of water.

Houses of people who were poor were made mostly from field stones packed with mud, which dried to a cement-like hardness. Roofs were made from reeds mixed with clay. These had to be replaced regularly. There was no indoor plumbing, of course.

In short, life for most people during the time of Jesus was a tough, daily struggle, with few comforts or luxuries. Jesus grew up and lived in this environment.

Two special influences on Jesus

In Judea, every sizable town had its own synagogue. The synagogue was the town's church and meeting hall. Jews would gather each Sabbath (Saturday) at the synagogue to hear the Scriptures and to listen to the rabbi (the religion teacher). They would sing hymns and offer prayers for the sick. Disputes would be settled. Important announcements were made. Collections would be taken to give to those who were poor and in need.

For devout Jews, the synagogue was the next best thing to the Temple itself. There they could pray, offer praise to God, and learn about God's Law. There they could be with their friends and forget about the Roman rulers.

Jesus was certainly a devout Jew. We can be sure he went regularly to the synagogue. Along with his family and friends, he sat on a bench and learned about God's Law. He prayed; he sang; he offered praise. He listened to the local rabbi's explanations. When he began his public life, Jesus gained the reputation of being a rabbi himself. He continued to go to the synagogue on the Sabbath in whatever town he was in. His own style of teaching was probably influenced by his childhood experiences in the synagogue in Nazareth.

When he came to Nazareth, where he had been brought up, he went to the synagogue on the sabbath day, as was his custom. He stood up to read, and the scroll of the prophet Isaiah was given to him. He unrolled the scroll and found the place where it was written:

"The Spirit of the Lord is upon me,
  because he has anointed me
    to bring good news to the poor.
He has sent me to proclaim release to the captives
    and recovery of sight to the blind,
      to let the oppressed go free,
    to proclaim the year of the Lord's favor."

And he rolled up the scroll, gave it back to the attendant, and sat down. The eyes of all in the synagogue were fixed on him. Then he began to say to them, "Today this scripture has been fulfilled in your hearing." All spoke well of him and were amazed at the gracious words that came from his mouth. (Luke 4:16–22)

CHECK IT OUT!

Jews of Jesus' time spoke Aramaic, a language that first came from Persia. Aramaic is now spoken in only one place in the world, a village called *Ma'lula* in the remote mountains of Syria.

Looking for Answers!

Check the correct reference.

The woman to whom Jesus spoke at a well was from the region of:

____ a. Matthew 15:21–28

____ b. Mark 6:21–34

____ c. Luke 10:38–41

____ d. John: 4:7–14

Answer: _____

CHECK IT OUT!

All Jewish boys were expected to learn to read so that they would be able to study and pray the Scriptures. There were "schools" for this purpose in almost every town in Palestine, including Nazareth.

How has the Church been part of your environment in growing up?

_____

_____

How has the Church influenced your thoughts and shaped who you are?

_____

_____

In addition to the synagogue, another important influence on Jesus was his parents. Unfortunately, the Gospels tell us very little about Mary, Jesus' mother. We know even less about Joseph, his foster father. But there are some things we can assume about them.

We know that Mary was specially loved and chosen by God to be the Mother of the Son of God through the power of the Holy Spirit. Like most women in her day, Mary was expected to be a wife, mother, and housekeeper. Her life was probably filled with the tasks of cooking, washing, sewing, tending to the needs of the family, visiting with neighbors and friends, going to the synagogue, and occasionally making a trip to the Temple. We know that Jesus obeyed her as a child and continued to respect her wishes as an adult. Jesus loved her deeply. To his dying breath, he was concerned for her.

Other than that, we don't know much. We can only imagine how she taught and trained Jesus, loved him and cared for him, washed his clothes and cooked his meals. In all these day-to-day events, Mary was undoubtedly shaping and molding Jesus the way any mother does. Seeing Jesus as a grown man is probably our best clue as to how well Mary did her job as a mother. Like her son, she must have been truly special.

Joseph, we know, was a carpenter. He probably taught Jesus his trade, the way fathers did in those days. He loved and protected Mary and Jesus. He provided them with a home and the necessities of life. He was a devout Jew, a just man. Perhaps the best clue we have about Joseph is Jesus' great love and devotion for his heavenly Father. This great reverence, and love for God is something Jesus undoubtedly learned by growing up under Joseph's care. So Joseph must have been an exceptionally good father!

CHECK IT OUT!

At the annunciation, Mary, though a virgin, miraculously conceived of Jesus by the power of the Holy Spirit. The Church teaches that Mary was conceived by her parents free from original sin through the power of God. Mary remained a virgin throughout her life. Mary is the Mother of God and is a model for the Church.

Scripture Search

As a class read Luke 2:41–52, a story about Jesus when he was twelve.

1. Why were Mary and Joseph looking for Jesus?

2. Where did they find him?

3. What was Jesus doing?

4. How would your parent(s)/guardian(s) feel if you were lost?

5. Where would they most likely find you? (Where is your favorite place to go?)

Which of your parents/guardians has had the greatest influence (positive or negative) on you? Why?
_____
_____
_____
_____

How would you describe your present relationship with your parent(s)/guardian(s)?
_____
_____
_____
_____
_____

The Call

Although he was the Son of God, Jesus was also truly human. To his friends and neighbors, Jesus probably seemed like any other young man living and working in Nazareth. He was a little more kind perhaps, a little more caring, a little more peaceful and self-disciplined. But certainly not the messiah everyone was looking for. But he had to earn a living, so that's what he did. Then came an event that changed all that.

Word spread throughout the land that a prophet named John the Baptizer was preaching in the deserts near the Jordan River south of Jerusalem. Jesus presented himself to be baptized by John. At that moment the heavens opened and a voice proclaimed, "You are my Son the Beloved; with you I am well pleased" (Luke 3:22).

After this experience, Jesus went away to pray and to prepare for his mission. He made a retreat in the desert near where he was baptized. He stayed there a number of days, praying. When he came back out of the desert, he began to proclaim the coming of God's reign.

Jesus didn't know if anyone would listen. He didn't know what might happen to him.

He knew that it was his mission to proclaim the good news of God's reign.

Jesus went back to his hometown of Nazareth a number of times after his baptism by John. But he never went back to his old life and trade. He was about thirty years old when he began to preach. Whenever he spoke, he brought with him all that he learned and experienced growing up in Nazareth. His teaching was filled with stories of farming, shepherding, and fishing. The covenant he had been taught as a child was the central theme behind what he now preached. Being poor and living with the poor gave Jesus a special understanding of those who were poor. Growing up in a nation that was ruled by invaders gave Jesus a special sympathy for the victims of bullies everywhere. In short, his childhood experiences in Nazareth helped to make him a very effective and easy-to-understand teacher.

CHECK IT OUT!

Some form of baptism has been used by many religions as a sign of cleansing or conversion or renewal. John the Baptizer didn't "invent" baptism, he redirected its meaning.

Scripture Search

When Jesus retreated to the desert to pray and prepare for his public life of ministry, he was tempted by the devil. To each temptation, Jesus responded with passages he had learned and knew from the Hebrew Scriptures. Read about the temptations of Jesus in Luke 4:1–13. Then match Jesus' responses with their correct passage in the Hebrew Scriptures.

_____ 1. Deuteronomy 6:16   A. "Man cannot live on bread alone."

_____ 2. Deuteronomy 8:3   B. "Worship the Lord your God and serve only him!"

_____ 3. Deuteronomy 6:13   C. "Do not put the Lord your God to the test."

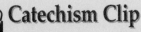

Getting to know Jesus

It's important to keep in mind that Jesus is truly God, the second Person of the Trinity. He was sent by God the Father to redeem humankind by the power of the Holy Spirit. Jesus is also a human being. Like you, he had to learn to talk, to walk, to say "please" and "thank you." When he skinned a knee playing, it hurt. When he got older and faced tough decisions, he had to struggle and to pray. It hurt him to be rejected or to hear people laugh when he was trying to teach them. He enjoyed a warm handshake, a cool drink of water, the smile of a friend. Jesus got tired after walking all day. He ached, sweated, and looked forward to taking a bath at the end of a long trip.

To get to know Jesus, then, means trying to keep in balance the fact that Jesus is truly God and truly human. How that is possible is a mystery none of us can hope to fully understand, but we know in faith that it's true.

Why is this so important? It's important because it means that Jesus, the Son of God, knows what it feels like to be tired, worried, afraid, and lonely. He's felt that way, too. The Son of God knows how great it feels to have friends around, to laugh at a good joke, to enjoy a good meal. It means that Jesus really understands you. It means that Jesus would also like you to understand him.

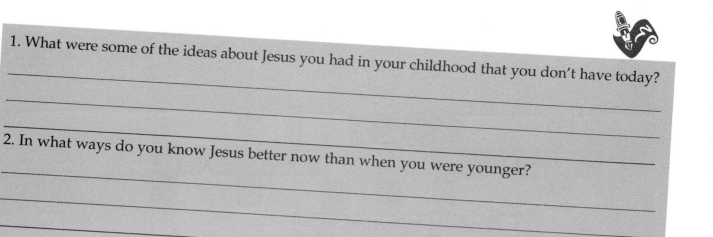

1. What were some of the ideas about Jesus you had in your childhood that you don't have today?

_____

_____

_____

2. In what ways do you know Jesus better now than when you were younger?

_____

_____

_____

Reflection

"Then he went down with them, and came to Nazareth, and was obedient to them. . . . And Jesus . . . increased in wisdom and in years and in divine and human favor." (Luke 12:51–52)

Briefly discuss how young people today can grow in wisdom and in divine and human favor.

Here is one way I will grow in friendship with Jesus this week:

_____

_____

_____

_____

Jesus,

Help me be obedient and respectful to my parents and to all those in authority.

Help me grow in wisdom, in knowledge of you, and in favor with God the Father and people.

Help me grow in friendship with you.

Amen.

Homework

Complete this crossword puzzle. Be prepared to go over the answers in class.

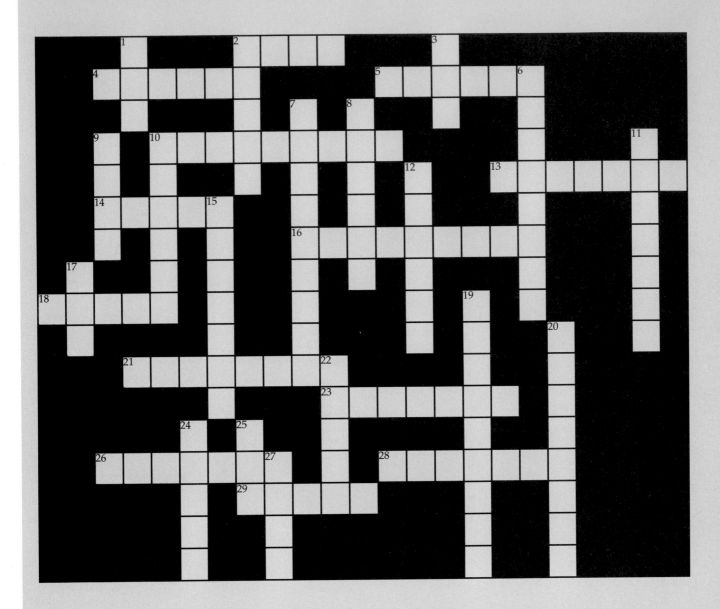

Across

2. the Baptizer
4. central place of Jewish worship in Jerusalem
5. The Jews are the _____ people.
10. location of the Temple
13. northern part of Palestine
14. received the Law from God
16. God's Word
18. Abraham was a man of _____ .
21. John was known as the _____ .
23. father of the Jewish people
26. Jesus proclaimed its coming.
28. built the first Temple
29. greatest king of Israel

Down

1. Jesus was a _____ .
2. the Son of God
3. Jesus was the _____ of Mary.
6. town where Jesus grew up
7. Jesus' country
8. Jesus went there to pray.
9. center of the empire in Jesus' day
10. Mary's husband
11. The Jewish people were looking for the _____ .
12. The Roman _____ controlled Palestine.
15. day of worship for the Jews
17. God gave Moses the _____ .
19. local gathering place for prayer and study
20. agreement between God and the Jewish people
22. religious teacher
24. the land Moses left
25. made a covenant with Abraham
27. Jesus' mother

A Personality Bigger than Life

Look at the pictures of Jesus on this page. Then, in a small group, discuss what YOU think Jesus looked like. Come to an agreement, if possible. Then work together to draw your image of Jesus on a separate sheet of paper. When you're done, share your picture/description of Jesus with the class.

 ## Catechism Clip

The first and last point of reference of this catechesis will always be Jesus Christ himself, who is "the way, and the truth, and the life." [Jn 14:6.] It is by looking to him in faith that Christ's faithful can hope that he himself fulfills his promises in them, and that, by loving him with the same love with which he has loved them, they may perform works in keeping with their dignity. . . . (1698)

What did Jesus look like?

There are no physical descriptions of Jesus in any of the Gospels or early Church writings. We have no photographs or statues that show how he actually looked. Maybe it's because Jesus was rather ordinary in appearance, a Jew among Jews.

But we do know this about Jesus: From the very first time he started to preach in public, he drew people to himself. In time, people came from all over Judea for a chance to hear him and meet him. Jesus held them so spellbound with his speaking that they would stay with him for hours, not thinking about where they were going to eat or sleep that night.

Everything Jesus did—from his gestures to his acceptance of dying on the cross—taught us something about who he was. There was something about this young rabbi from Nazareth that touched people deep inside. In a way, you could say he had a personality bigger than life.

In this chapter, we're going to look closer at the personality of Jesus. We'll look at some reasons why Jesus was able to draw people to himself and experience them as his friends.

Jesus was approachable

Imagine yourself living back in first-century Galilee. Jesus comes to your town with his followers. Eagerly, you and your friends join the crowd that has gathered to hear Jesus speak. You make your way through the crowd, and finally you see Jesus for yourself. What do you observe?

Probably the first thing you'd notice is how approachable Jesus is. You'd see how everybody could come right up to him. They don't have to be important. They don't have to get an appointment or go through a number of secretaries. Maybe they'd have to wait their turn, but Jesus would eventually welcome them. You'd see an old man come to him, a sick woman, a mother with her baby. Young people your age would walk right up to Jesus, and he would chat with them. You'd see public sinners, beggars, even lepers come out of the crowd and approach Jesus. He would welcome them just like everyone else.

CHECK IT OUT!

The term *lepers* included anyone with a skin rash or skin disease. It didn't always mean people who had the actual disease of leprosy.

You'd also see that Jesus didn't have much time to himself as a result. Maybe he'd be teaching in someone's house. Men would literally take the roof off the house so they could lower their paralyzed friend down in front of Jesus. Jesus wouldn't get angry or complain about being interrupted. He'd stop his teaching and attend to the man who was sick. As you follow along with the crowd, you'd probably see how his disciples would try to keep someone who was begging away so he or she wouldn't bother Jesus. But each time Jesus caught on to what his disciples were doing, he'd stop them and welcome the beggar.

Like most people in the crowd, you'd wonder how Jesus could remain so calm and patient, so friendly and attentive in all the hubbub and noise. You'd marvel at how he could keep going as the day grew hotter and he grew tired. But all day long, you'd see how Jesus continued to be approachable. You'd see how people weren't afraid to keep coming to him. After watching for an hour or so, chances are you wouldn't be afraid to approach him, either.

Jesus' Miracles

Throughout his ministry, Jesus worked several different types of miracles. The first type can be called spiritual miracles and are perhaps the greatest of all. In these miracles, we see Jesus touching people's hearts, not their bodies.

Some of Jesus' healing miracles were physical miracles. He could directly heal the body, not just the mind. Often Jesus cured from a distance, without even coming into contact with the person.

Scripture shows Jesus performing a third kind of miracle, certain nature miracles. This means he showed great power over natural forces. Such miracles show that Jesus was sent by God the Father. Not only did Jesus have power over nature, he also had power to save people from the power of sin and death.

The Gospels are filled with stories about the miracles Jesus performed. In small groups read each of the stories listed below. Then place a check mark in the column that you feel fits the type of miracle performed. You may decide that a miracle fits into two columns.

	Spiritual	Physical	Nature
Matthew 8:23–27			
Mark 2:1–12			
Mark 5:25–34			
Mark 6:45–52			
Mark 7:31–37			
Luke 6:6–10			
Luke 7:1–10			
Luke 7:36–50			
Luke 9:10–17			
Luke 17:11–19			
Luke 19:1–10			
John 2:1–11			
John 8:1–11			

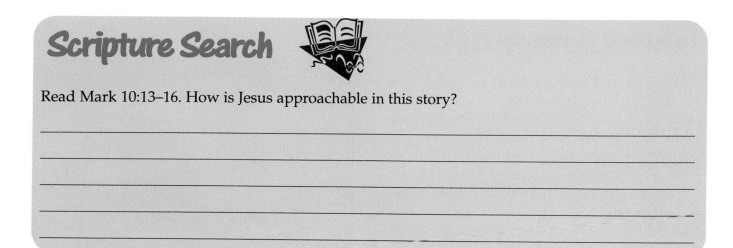

Scripture Search

Read Mark 10:13–16. How is Jesus approachable in this story?

_____

_____

_____

_____

_____

Fill in the following chart. Give an example of how each of the persons mentioned is approachable. For each example, name a result—something that happened or happens because of the action.

APPROACHABLE

Person	Example	Result
Jesus		
Someone I admire		

Here are some ways I can imitate Jesus and be approachable:

_____

_____

_____

Jesus was respectful

Let's go back to first-century Galilee. You've climbed up on an ox cart now, so you can see over the crowd. As you watch different people come up to Jesus, you'd probably begin to notice how respectfully Jesus treats each person.

You can tell this by the way Jesus looks at each person. You can tell by the way he talks to a woman who is elderly or puts his arm around someone who is begging. You can tell by the way he takes time with people and really listens when they tell him something.

Jesus' attitude, you notice, is more than routine politeness. It's surely not that phony interest in others that some politicians show when they're working the crowd. What begins to come across to you is the fact that Jesus sincerely values and honors each person. No matter how busy or tired he is, Jesus treats each person—regardless of wealth, looks, clothes, age, or public reputation—as a truly unique and important individual. It's as if Jesus looks deep within each person he meets and then, just as deeply, loves and values what he finds there.

By the end of the day, it would probably become very clear to you that Jesus really believes and practices what he teaches: Every human is a son or daughter of God; every person is a priceless, unique, and valued individual. You'd see people who were never once in their whole life treated with any real respect go away with a new attitude toward themselves and toward life. You'd see people—after meeting Jesus just once—begin to believe in themselves for the first time.

By the end of the day, you'd probably find yourself caught up in that same spirit. Jesus' obvious love and respect for each person would begin to "infect" you, too. We work with God's kingdom whenever we follow the words and example of Jesus. You'd feel differently about your own worth, your own value and importance in God's eyes. That seems to be the effect Jesus had on people as he moved from town to town. He respected everyone, and they learned to respect themselves.

CHECK IT OUT!

Perhaps Henry Ward Beecher had Jesus in mind when he wrote:

"There are persons so radiant, so genial, so kind, so pleasure-bearing, that you instinctively feel in their presence that they do you good, whose coming into a room is like the bringing of a lamp there."

Scripture Search

Jesus respected everyone, regardless of their wealth, looks, clothes, age, or public reputation. From memory, name some examples from the New Testament that show Jesus treating someone with respect (an example: Luke 19:1–10).

In our world today, where is there a need for greater respect for people?

Fill in the following chart. Give an example of how each of the persons mentioned are respectful of others. For each example, name a result—something that happened or happens because of the action.

RESPECTFUL

Person	Example	Result
Jesus		
Someone I admire		

Here are some ways I can imitate Jesus and be respectful of others:

_____

_____

_____

Jesus was concerned

Let's return to Galilee. You've worked your way to the front of the crowd. You're almost right in front of Jesus. He's talking to a man whose daughter is sick. The man is frantic with worry and is asking Jesus to come to his house. This time what's obvious to you is that Jesus is clearly feeling the pain and fear of the father. He's able to identify with the man, to get involved. Concern is in his eyes, in his voice, in his facial expression.

CHECK IT OUT!

In Jesus' time, people didn't have hospitals as we think of them today. Doctors had very limited abilities. The best ones could do some simple surgery, though, and had a good knowledge of the medical powers of various herbs.

Jesus agrees to go with the father to see the child. The crowd—and you—go off with Jesus toward the man's house. On the way, an old woman jostles her way through the crowd, gets behind Jesus and tugs on his robe. He stops, looks around, and sees her. In her face is a plea for help. She has some lifelong sickness.

Again, you can see that concern in Jesus' eyes. He's deeply moved by the woman's faith and by her problem. He takes time out to attend to her needs. He doesn't say "Come back later" or "Wait your turn."

In spending just one day with Jesus, you'd probably begin to realize how sincerely he identified with the people around him. The last thing anyone could ever call Jesus is "detached" or "indifferent" or "uninterested." He wasn't afraid to show his sadness, express his feelings, or even cry when he saw someone suffering. But Jesus never stopped there. He got practical. He got involved. He did whatever he thought was best to help the person. Jesus' concerns for other people went a step further. His words and actions invited belief in him and in God the Father who had sent him.

CHECK IT OUT!

"There is much satisfaction in work well done; praise is sweet; but there can be no happiness equal to the joy of finding a heart that understands."
—Victor Robinsoll

Scripture Search

Jesus showed great concern and understanding for all people. Read the story about the widow's son in Luke 7:11–15. Out of concern and pity for the widow, what does Jesus do?

Fill in the following chart. Give an example of how each of the persons mentioned is concerned about others. For each example, name a result—something that happened or happens because of the action.

CONCERNED

Person	Example	Result
Jesus		
Someone I admire		

Here are some ways I can imitate Jesus and show concern for others:
_____
_____
_____

Jesus was humble

Let's suppose on the day Jesus came through your town, he not only cured some people, but he also performed some miraculous feat. Perhaps he fed 5,000 people with a few loaves of bread. Perhaps he calmed a storm or walked across the Sea of Galilee.

Without doubt, you'd feel the awe and the excitement in the crowd. You'd hear the "ohs" and "ahs" of wonder. And you'd sense this is no ordinary man. You'd see Jesus as someone whose word is being backed up by God himself.

All this gets you thinking further. Who is Jesus really? When he does something wonderful, he doesn't try to show off or use his powers to impress people with how important he is. He doesn't try to get the crowd to make him their leader. He never asks anything for himself. It seems that, especially when he performs a miracle, Jesus keeps trying to focus people's attention on God, whom he calls Father, and on the covenant the Jewish people have with God.

After only one day of watching Jesus, it would be rather clear to you that Jesus was a messenger of God the Father, someone sent to speak and teach and heal in God's name. The power to work miracles was given to Jesus by the Father. It was proof, to anyone with the eyes of faith, that Jesus truly was chosen by God the Father to be his spokesman. In other words, he was commissioned by God the Father.

CHECK IT OUT!

Humility does not mean putting yourself down. Rather, it means giving credit where credit is due. Every talent and ability we have comes from God, not from ourselves.

Catechism Clip

Jesus accompanies his words with many "mighty works and wonders and signs," which manifest that the kingdom is present in him and attest that he was the promised Messiah [Acts 2:22; cf. Lk 7:18–23]. The signs worked by Jesus attest that the Father has sent him. They invite belief in him [Cf. Jn 5:36; 10:25, 38]. (547, 548)

CHECK IT OUT!

In Jesus' words: "For all who exalt themselves will be humbled, and those who humble themselves will be exalted." (Luke 14:11)

The Sea of Galilee

Scripture Search

Read aloud Philippians 2:5–11. Discuss the following questions as a class.

What does this passage teach us about the humility of Jesus?

What does it mean that "the same mind must be in you that was in Christ Jesus"?

Fill in the following chart. Give an example of how each of the persons mentioned is humble. For each example, name a result—something that happened or happens because of the action.

HUMBLE

Person	Example	Result
Jesus		
Someone I admire		

Here are some ways I can imitate Jesus and be humble:

_____

_____

_____

Reflection

"[Jesus] went up the mountain, where he sat down. Great crowds came to him, bringing with them the lame, the maimed, the blind, the mute, and many others. They put them at his feet, and he cured them. . . ." (Matthew 15:29–30)

Jesus once said that those who have faith could work even greater miracles than he did. Briefly discuss ways that young people today can work "miracles" with others.

Here is one way I will imitate Jesus this week:

_____

_____

Jesus,

Help me be approachable and make people around me feel comfortable and at ease.

Help me be humble and respect and care for others—especially those who are poor, elderly, and lonely.

Help me realize that I am a unique, valued child of God and act accordingly.

Amen.

Homework

Be prepared to discuss the following questions:

• What quality of Jesus appeals to you the most? Why?

• Do you believe miracles can still happen today? Why or why not?

• If God chose to come to earth today in human form, what do you think that human form would look like? Bring to the next class an original drawing, poem, or song that explains what you mean.

4

Have I Got News for You!

Think about the last time a friend phoned you or wrote you a letter and told you something you didn't know before. That news was not only a surprise, something new, it also changed your life in some small way. Perhaps it changed the way you thought about someone. Maybe it changed the way you felt about a situation. Or perhaps it even inspired you to make a change in your own behavior.

News and change go hand in hand. Some news results in only small changes, changes so subtle or so slow we hardly notice them. Other news—such as the ability to clone animals—is so great, so dramatic, and so unexpected, that we call it revolutionary.

Form a group with two or three others. Discuss these questions:

- What was the worst news you've had all week?

- How did that news affect, or change, you?

- What was the best news you've had all week?

- How did that news affect, or change, you?

- If you could make one dramatic change in today's world, what change would you make? Why?

The good news of Jesus was not subtle or small. It was a gigantic surprise, something totally unexpected and dramatic. In fact, we could say that the good news of Jesus was revolutionary. It changed almost everything.

CHECK IT OUT!

The dictionary defines *revolution* as a sudden, radical, or complete change.

39

Jesus turned things upside down

Jesus wasn't revolutionary in the popular way we now use the word in newspaper headlines. He didn't stir up crowds against the government. He didn't command a guerrilla army in the hills of Galilee. He didn't lead terrorist attacks on Roman garrisons. But like any revolutionary, he turned things upside down.

Jesus turned upside down people's way of looking at life. He went to the root of things. He challenged the ideas, values, and "truths" upon which people built societies. Jesus proclaimed a whole new vision of what human life is all about. Ultimately, what Jesus turned upside down were people's hearts and minds.

You've grown up hearing most of Jesus' sayings, teachings, and "rules" for living. This news may seem "old" or stale to you. And news that's two thousand years old hardly seems revolutionary. But that's your challenge in this course: to rediscover just how revolutionary Jesus was and how revolutionary it is, even today, to be a follower of Jesus.

So let's go back to the time Jesus first started teaching. Let's try to imagine that the ideas you hear him saying are ideas you've never heard before. Try to put aside all you've been told and all you've heard about Jesus when you were a little child. Try to imagine that you're a Jewish youth back in Galilee at the time Jesus first started to teach.

Prepare yourself! Jesus is about to turn upside down the way you think about God and religion!

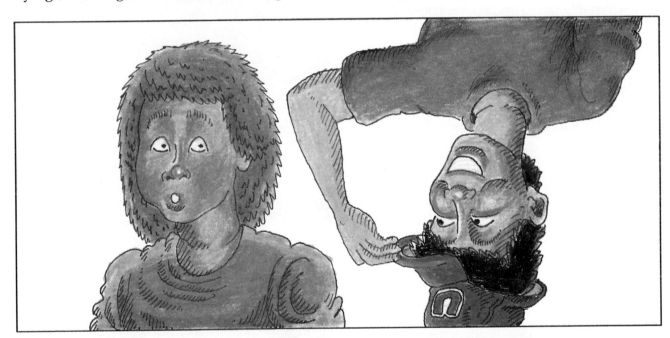

1. Some ideas I presently have about God include:

_____

_____

2. Some ideas I presently have about religion include:

_____

_____

40

Images of God

To help you get into the minds of Jewish people more than two thousand years ago, read the following Scripture passages. What image of God do these Scripture passages present? What kind of feelings would you have toward such a God?

Scripture	Kind of God	My Feelings
Genesis 3		
Exodus 19:16–25		
2 Samuel 6:1–10		
Psalm 7:7–14		
Psalm 62		

Discuss your findings with the class. Then take a piece of drawing paper or poster board. Divide it in half. On one side, make a collage of images that represent God as the Jewish people of two thousand years ago thought of him.

The God of Jesus

Devout Jews in Jesus' time had a holy fear, or reverence, of God. Because of this reverence, they never even spoke God's name. Their idea was that God was so powerful, so holy, so just, and so all-knowing that they needed to keep a respectful distance. True, their God wasn't cruel or selfish like many of the Roman and Greek gods. But their God could get very angry and could dish out some pretty big punishments.

CHECK IT OUT!

Jewish people were forbidden by the Law from making statues or pictures to represent God.

The Jews did believe that God was concerned for them. Devout Jews would pray to God with confidence. But many still tended to approach him with caution. They had a real fear of doing anything that might offend and anger him.

Then Jesus came along. From the start, he talked about and related to God in a unique way. Jesus described God as "Abba." In the Aramaic language that Jesus and his fellow Jews spoke, "Abba" was the affectionate term children used when addressing their father.

What news this was! Jesus was saying that the awesome, fearsome, all-holy God was a loving Father! This news upset some people. To many others, it was a scandal.

But Jesus didn't stop there. He said that each person is a special, precious child of God and has the right to approach God as Abba. Jesus encouraged EVERYONE (man, woman, child, elderly person, Jew, Roman, Greek) to approach God in a childlike, familiar, affectionate, and trusting way. Jesus taught that God, like all good parents, is concerned about and involved in all aspects of our lives.

Images of God, continued

Fill in the second half of the drawing paper or poster board with a collage that represents God the Father as Jesus spoke of him.

If God is "Abba" to everyone, then God loves all people, even the ones we dislike or don't get along with. Think about someone you dislike. How do you think God sees this person? What change does this good news about God challenge you to make?

_____

_____

_____

📎 Catechism Clip

When we pray to "our" Father, we personally address the Father of our Lord Jesus Christ. . . . if we pray the Our Father sincerely, we leave individualism behind. . . . The "our" at the beginning of the Lord's Prayer . . . excludes no one. If we are to say it truthfully, our divisions and oppositions have to be overcome. [Cf. Mt 5:23–24; 6:14–15.] (2789, 2792)

Looking for Answers!

Jesus addresses God as Abba in which two of the following passages:

____ a. Matthew 6:22–23

____ b. Mark 14:36

____ c. 2 Thessalonians 2:16–17

____ d. Romans 8:14–16

Activity

Jesus taught his followers that God should be called *Abba*, a loving Father. When you pray to God, how do you address him? From the list below, choose three ways you are most likely to address God. After each choice, list possible times in life when you would address God this way.

____ Father of Mercy	____ Our Counselor
____ Rock of Safety	____ God of Truth
____ Great Shepherd	____ Strength to the Needy
____ Author of our Faith	____ Awesome God
____ Father of Peace	____ The Just One
____ God of the Whole Earth	____ God of All Grace
____ God, Full of Compassion	____ Our Confidence
____ Our Advocate	____ God of Justice
____ Our Hope	____ Creator of All
____ Mighty God	____ Source of All Holiness

Choice #1: _____

_____

Choice #2: _____

_____

Choice #3: _____

_____

Religious Rules

Jesus also had news about religious rules. He taught that what's really important in approaching Abba is what's in our hearts. Jesus didn't attack religious practices and religious rules, as such. In fact, he said they were important. But he reminded us that religious laws and practices don't have any value unless our hearts are in the right place.

Many devout Jews, following the instructions of some of their religious leaders, had come to put a great deal of importance on external rules and practices. Keeping the smallest law was seen as a way to ensure that the greater laws would receive their proper respect. However, some people thought that even one little slip up—like forgetting to say a particular prayer or wash a cup in a certain way—could make them "unclean" in God's eyes.

CHECK IT OUT!

In addition to the Ten Commandments, the Jewish people were expected to keep the 613 laws of Moses.

Jesus said that having a clean heart was much more important than not eating without washing your hands. He said that it didn't make much sense to keep a religious rule if, at the same time, you were cheating your friend, bullying the people around you, or lying to your parents. Jesus called that kind of action hypocrisy. He even accused some of the Jewish leaders of being phonies. They were pious rule-keepers in public, but they were selfish and self-serving in private.

. . . and the large crowd was listening to Jesus with delight. As he taught, he said, "Beware of the scribes, who like to walk around in long robes, and to be greeted with respect in the marketplaces, and to have the best seats in the synagogues and places of honor at banquets. They devour widows' houses, and for the sake of appearances say long prayers. They will receive the greater condemnation." (Mark 12:37–40)

Then [Jesus] called the crowd to him and said to them, "Listen and understand: it is not what goes into the mouth that defiles a person, but it is what comes out of the mouth that defiles. . . . Do you not see that whatever goes into the mouth enters the stomach, and goes out into the sewer? But what comes out of the mouth proceeds from the heart, and this is what defiles. For out of the heart come evil intentions, murder, adultery, fornication, theft, false witness, slander. These are what defile a person, but to eat with unwashed hands does not defile." (Matthew 15:10–11, 17–20)

Not only was Jesus revolutionary in terms of what he was saying about the Jewish Law, he also challenged the right of some of the Jewish leaders to be leaders. He even warned the people to beware of some leaders' false ideas.

Remember, you are a devout Jewish youth hearing all this for the first time. As a Jew, your religion—with its Law, its Temple, and its religious leaders—is the single most important authority in the world. Jesus, this upstart carpenter-turned-rabbi, is challenging what you've been taught to think is important. He's threatening your whole world. And yet he makes sense. That's revolutionary!

CHECK IT OUT!

The Talmud promotes understanding of Judaism. It is the official book that contains the rules and religious customs that flow from the Torah, the Law of Moses or the Law of the Covenant. The rules contained in the Talmud cover just about every detail of life and right living.

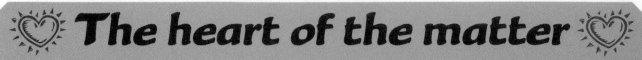

The heart of the matter

Here is a list of the Ten Commandments from Deuteronomy 5:6–21. In a small group, read each commandment and discuss what it means. Then give one example of how young people today can keep this commandment in their actions and "in their hearts."

First commandment: I am the Lord your God. You shall have no other gods before me.

Example: _____

_____

Second commandment: Do not take the name of the Lord your God in vain.

Example: _____

_____

Third commandment: Keep holy the Lord's day.

Example: _____

_____

Fourth commandment: Honor your father and mother.

Example: _____

_____

Fifth commandment: Do not kill.

Example: _____

_____

Sixth commandment: Do not commit adultery.

Example: _____

_____

Seventh commandment: Do not steal.

Example: _____

_____

Eighth commandment: Do not lie about your neighbor.

Example: _____

_____

Ninth commandment: Do not covet your neighbor's wife.

Example: _____

_____

Tenth commandment: Do not covet your neighbor's possessions.

Example: _____

_____

God's kingdom of peace

Jesus wasn't revolutionary just in terms of the Jewish religion. He also challenged the values and common sense principles of the world at large.

Many Jewish people were awaiting a messiah who would reestablish the kingdom of David. They thought of this kingdom much like the Romans thought of their empire. This kingdom would give the Jewish people new status and power. They would no longer be pushed around by neighboring countries. It would be a kingdom with great wealth and fame. Other nations would look up to this kingdom with envy.

Some of the Jews believed that the messiah's kingdom on earth was only for Jews, only for devout, God-fearing, Covenant-obeying Jews. Sinners and those who didn't follow the religious practices would be tossed out. Enemies would be punished or even destroyed.

But Jesus brought different news about God's kingdom. Here are some of the things Jesus said:

- In God's kingdom, people are not divided into friends and enemies. In fact, people will live in peace with one another. They will forgive their enemies, rather than hate them. "But I say to you, Love your enemies and pray for those who persecute you" (Matthew 5:44).

- In God's kingdom, people do not seek revenge when they are wronged. Instead, they will be patient and will turn the other cheek. "But I say to you, Do not resist an evildoer. But if anyone strikes you on the right cheek, turn the other also" (Matthew 5:39).

- Detachment from riches is necessary for entering the kingdom of God. "Sell your possessions, and give alms. Make purses for yourselves that do not wear out, an unfailing treasure in heaven, where no thief comes near and no moth destroys. For where your treasure is, there your heart will be also" (Luke 12:33–34).

- God's kingdom will not be fully realized here on earth. The fullness of the kingdom will be reached only at the second coming. At the end of time, all those who have died in Christ will share in the new creation. ". . . in fact Christ has been raised from the dead, the first fruits of those who have died. For since death came through a human being, the resurrection of the dead must come through a human being; for as all die in Adam, so all will be made alive in Christ" (1 Corinthians 15:20–22).

47

What would a follower of Jesus do?

Form a small group with several others. Choose one of the following situations to role play for the class. After each situation, discuss possible ways that a follower of Christ might respond.

Situation 1: You live in a neighborhood that has several gangs in it. Last night, the rival gang spray-painted the fences and garage doors of two members of your gang. Those members want your gang to retaliate tonight. What do you say/do?

Situation 2: Your parents have just gotten divorced. They "hate" each other and still fight whenever they are on the phone together. Your parents are trying to make you take sides and choose one parent over the other. What do you say/do?

Situation 3: You are standing in a long line at the movie theater. You just about get up to the ticket booth when two teenagers (older and bigger) cut in line in front of you. What do you say/do?

Situation 4: Your younger sister borrowed your favorite sweatshirt without you knowing it. Now you find it wadded up in the bottom of your drawer with a hideous stain on the front. What do you say/do?

Situation 5: A friend tries to get you to sell drugs with him. He says it's a fast way to make lots of money, and that's all that counts in life. What do you say/do?

Situation 6: In private, your friends like to make fun of people who have handicaps. They want nothing to do with the new girl in class, who has braces on her legs. What do you say/do?

Blessed are the poor

Contrary to some popular ideas of his day, Jesus said that being rich didn't count for much in God's kingdom. Instead of the rich, it was the poor who would be blessed and happy. Being powerful, famous, and in control of others didn't count for much, either, in God's kingdom. Instead, Jesus suggested that the meek, the peacemakers, and the victims of unjust persecution would be the ones who were honored. Jesus went on to say that if someone really wanted to be in charge, he or she should become the servant of others. Power and wealth should be used to help others, not as a means of controlling them.

More disturbing news: Jesus told his listeners that everyone could enter God's kingdom. Everyone would be welcome, those who are poor along with those who are rich, those who are enslaved along with those who are free, people of other lands along with the Jews. In fact, most of the outcasts in society—those who were poor, uneducated, sick, disabled, elderly, and sinful—had a good chance of being the first to take their place in God's realm.

When people heard Jesus talking like this, many thought he was foolish. It went against just about every principle of common sense that ever existed. Everybody knew that to be rich and powerful was to "have it made." To be poor and weak was to be a "loser."

Everybody knew that the only way to treat enemies was to get even with them or even destroy them.

Jesus didn't back down, however, and he didn't water down his message. Many people who were rich and powerful hated him for what he was saying. His ideas were a dangerous threat to their position in society. Many of the middle class who were attempting to become rich and powerful didn't like Jesus, either. He was upsetting their plans.

So you can guess who was most attracted to Jesus: Those who were poor and oppressed, the "losers" in society. They became Jesus' most faithful followers. His message—now called the *Beatitudes*—gave them hope. No one else in society, not even the religious leaders, had ever given them such dignity. This was indeed revolutionary!

To take such news seriously meant to turn upside down all the goals and values of human society throughout history. But the followers of Jesus did take the news seriously. And they still do. That's why true Christians are just as revolutionary today as Jesus was two thousand years ago. The message Jesus was offering to the people of his time still confronts us today with decisive choices concerning possessions. Jesus asks us to purify our hearts in order to love God above all things.

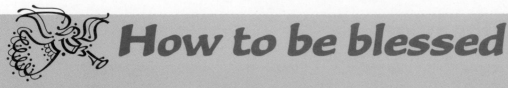

How to be blessed

Jesus gave his followers a revolutionary new formula. We call this formula the Beatitudes. Form a team of three or four. Together, read Matthew 5:1–12. Then rewrite the Beatitudes in language (a poem, rap song, and so on) that would make sense to young people today. When you're finished, share with the class what you've written.

_____ (title)

_____

_____

_____

_____

_____

_____

_____

1. Do you think it is still revolutionary to follow Jesus today? Why or why not?

_____

_____

2. What I find most attractive about Jesus' message is:

_____

_____

CHECK IT OUT!

The world now has almost six billion people in it. Each year, 15–20 million of them die of starvation or of diseases related to malnutrition. That's 41,000 people every day, 28 deaths every minute.

Imagine

- Imagine right now the kingdom of God in its fullness. What is it like?
- Imagine yourself going into the Pentagon and announcing that power isn't important. What do you think would happen?
- Imagine going to Wall Street and shouting out that wealth doesn't make a person important or guarantee happiness. How do you think people would respond to you?

The point is this: Jesus' message about God's kingdom is as revolutionary today as it was two thousand years ago. Many people have never really heard it. Many others have heard it but don't think it makes sense.

Right now, you are at a crossroads in your life. The direction you take now will play a big part in determining how you'll spend the rest of your life. Jesus was revolutionary. If you decide to become a mature, dedicated follower of Jesus, you are choosing to be revolutionary, too. It might turn out to be a rough path at times, just as it was for Jesus. But at least you'll know you're traveling in good company.

"Blessed are the poor in spirit, for theirs is the kingdom of heaven. . . . Blessed are the meek, for they will inherit the earth. . . . Blessed are the peacemakers, for they will be called children of God."
(Matthew 5:3, 5, 9)

Briefly discuss how we can live the Beatitudes today.

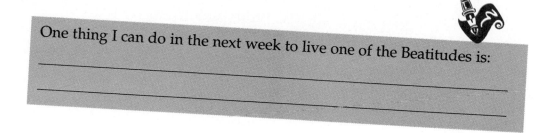

One thing I can do in the next week to live one of the Beatitudes is:

_____

_____

Jesus,

Help me live the Beatitudes.

Help me accept the challenge of being a Christian today.

Help me be faith-filled and joy-filled so that others may see you in me.

Help me keep my eyes on the kingdom of God.

Amen.

Homework

You have been chosen to give a speech to a group of your peers about how young Christians are called to be revolutionary in their thoughts, words, and actions. In your speech you need to describe for the teenage audience what it means to be revolutionary, including examples of what this would mean in their homes, schools, parishes, and communities. At some point in your speech, you need to include two quotes from Jesus. Look through the New Testament (especially the Gospels) for possibilities or feel free to use the passages mentioned in this chapter. Begin your brainstorming below. Write your final draft on a separate piece of paper. Your speech should last two to four minutes. Be prepared to present your work to your class.

Ideas I'd like to include:

• Homes:

• Schools:

• Parishes:

• Communities

Two quotes from Jesus:

5

One Day at a Time

Then and Now

How does your life compare with the time when Jesus lived? What differences do you imagine exist from then to now regarding clothing, food, shelter, transportation, and money? Form small groups and discuss what you believe to be true of Jesus' time and what is true now. Jot your ideas below. Be ready to share with the rest of the class.

Clothing
Time of Jesus:

Now:

Food
Time of Jesus:

Now:

Shelter
Time of Jesus:

Now:

Transportation
Time of Jesus:

Now:

Money
Time of Jesus:

Now:

Day-to-day holiness

Sometimes people think that becoming a saint (someone who is holy) means achieving something extraordinary. It's true that some saints founded religious communities or schools. Others gave their lives as missionaries in far-away countries. Some saints went to heroic measures to provide food and clothing for those who were poor or to achieve justice for those who were oppressed. But most saints are ordinary people who follow Jesus to the best of their ability in ordinary day-to-day situations.

This is certainly one of the messages of Jesus: Holiness is found in the ordinary; everyone is called to be holy. One way that Jesus announced this good news was by his own example, by the way he lived.

Do you ever wonder what the day-to-day life of Jesus was like? The Gospels don't tell us much about that. But we can form some idea about his life by reading between the lines of the Gospels and by becoming familiar with how people in Palestine lived 2000 years ago.

Clothing. Jesus probably dressed like any other working-class person of his day. This meant wearing leather sandals and a simple, rough-woven tunic with a leather or rope belt and a heavier outer robe that doubled as a blanket at night. Like the poorer class, Jesus wouldn't have many changes of clothes, so he didn't have much to carry with him as he traveled the country. It's possible that Jesus had to take time out from his teaching and healing on occasion to do his laundry!

Food. When they traveled, Jesus and his disciples often cooked their food on a campfire. When Jesus was in a town, friends or local officials sometimes invited him to eat a meal with them. He accepted these invitations and often used them as opportunities to teach.

Sometimes followers brought food to Jesus and his disciples when they stayed in the country-side. Eating was a necessity that Jesus seemed to deal with one day at a time. As Matthew tells us, sometimes Jesus and his disciples went to sleep hungry (Matthew 12:1–8).

Shelter. Jesus slept outdoors much of the time, especially when he was teaching in the countryside. He and his disciples would simply camp out, sleeping on the ground around a campfire or sleeping on a boat on the Sea of Galilee. Friends and followers would invite Jesus to spend the night at their house if he was in a town. Often, this meant sleeping in their courtyard, an open area attached to the house. Once Jesus started his ministry, he probably didn't spend too many nights sleeping in a real bed.

Transportation. Jesus and his disciples covered many miles in their ministry, and their main mode of transportation was their feet. Whether it was getting around the region of Galilee or traveling south to the Temple in Jerusalem, they walked. Only on special occasions or out of necessity did people in Jesus' time use a donkey to transport themselves or cargo. They used boats to cross bodies of water.

CHECK IT OUT!

Jesus is described several times in the Gospels as having his feet uncovered (Luke 7:38; Luke 24:40; John 12:3).

Money. Disciples who followed Jesus full-time chipped in to the common purse whatever money they brought with them. Devoted followers gave the group money when they passed through town. Jesus didn't seem to have any plan for raising money, and we never find him asking for money for himself in the Gospels. As he so often taught his followers, Jesus seemed to rely upon God's goodness for whatever he needed.

When it comes to necessities then, it's good to remember that Jesus had to take care of day-to-day needs just like anyone else. These day-to-day needs didn't distract Jesus from his love for God the Father or his ability to serve others. Instead, they were opportunities for Jesus to experience God the Father and grow in holiness. They were times when Jesus helped others to find God's love and to grow in holiness, too.

Looking for Answers!

Check the correct reference.

An occasion on which a donkey was used for transportation was:

___ a. Mark 13:1–4

___ b. Matthew 21:1–9

___ c. John 12:44–50

___ d. Luke 3:21–22

The occasion: _____

55

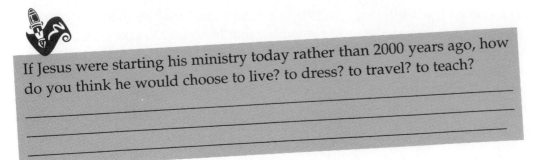

If Jesus were starting his ministry today rather than 2000 years ago, how do you think he would choose to live? to dress? to travel? to teach?

_____

_____

_____

CHECK IT OUT!

The most common coin in Jesus' time was a silver denarius, worth about sixteen cents in our current money. Read Matthew 26:14–16. In our current money, what would be the worth of Judas' betrayal of Jesus?

Scripture Search

Read Matthew 6:26–34. In a small group, discuss what this Scripture passage means. Then discuss the following questions.

1. What are some things young people today worry about?

2. Is it good advice to "Stop worrying"? Explain.

3. What are some ordinary situations in which young people today can experience God's love and grow in holiness?

4. What are some ordinary times in which young people today can help others to find God's love and to grow in holiness?

Here are two ordinary times/situations this week when I will open myself to God's love and grow in holiness:

_____

_____

Here are two ordinary times/situations this week when I will try to help others find God's love and grow in holiness:

_____

_____

Starting with the ordinary

One of the reasons Jesus was such a memorable teacher was that he employed effective teaching techniques. First of all, Jesus started his lessons with the ordinary experiences of the people who were listening to him. Jesus began with something his listeners already knew. Then he built on that. He taught people something new about God's love and God's kingdom.

Second, Jesus adapted the good news to the particular situation of his listeners—their local geography, jobs, and daily interests. For example, if Jesus was near a seaport or lake where most of the people engaged in fishing for a living, he explained God's kingdom in terms of fishing. If Jesus was talking to a group of housewives, he explained God's kingdom in terms of making bread, keeping a clean house, and delighting in the presence of children. If Jesus spoke in the countryside, he explained God's kingdom in terms of farming and shepherding. If he spoke to business persons in one of the towns along the trade routes, he explained God's kingdom in terms of investing wisely and making money.

Third, Jesus captured the attention of his listeners by using stories, or parables, from ordinary life. People were interested in these stories because the main characters were people just like themselves. People listened to Jesus because they wanted to find out how the stories ended.

One of the most famous parables of Jesus is the Parable of the Forgiving Father, also known as the Parable of the Prodigal Son (Luke 15:11–32). Read the parable. Then discuss these questions:

- What is the ordinary setting of this parable?

- What kinds of people were probably listening to Jesus when he told this parable?

- Who are the main characters in the parable? Why do you think people identified with them?

- Which character in the parable do you identify with? Why?

- What do you think Jesus was trying to say about God's kingdom through this parable?

- How does this parable apply to us today?

Simple things

Early in his public ministry, Jesus traveled to Capernaum, a bustling city on the shore of the Sea of Galilee. There, he talked to people whose lives consisted of fairly simple things. They either fished or tended house or had small businesses.

Jesus didn't have some detailed plan about where he would go to preach and heal on a particular day or week. He often "played it by ear," responding to the Spirit. It was much the same in terms of the words he used to teach. Yet his basic message was always the same: Our God is Abba, a kind and loving Father; the kingdom of God, in which everyone is valued and accepted, is coming soon. Beyond that, what Jesus taught and how he taught it often depended on the situations in which he found himself.

For instance, suppose Jesus was at the supper table of a person who was rich and the guests were maneuvering to get the places of honor. Jesus would take that opportunity to teach about the nature and importance of humility. Suppose Jesus was passing by a vineyard where the workers were trimming the vines. He'd stop, turn to his followers and tell them a parable using the vineyard as his theme. If Jesus was by the seashore when the fishermen were dragging in their nets, he'd describe how the kingdom of God was like a net and the people were like the fish caught up in it.

 Catechism Clip

Jesus' invitation to enter his kingdom comes in the form of parables, a characteristic feature of his teaching. [Cf. Mk 4:33–34.] Through his parables he invites people to the feast of the kingdom, but he also asks for a radical choice: to gain the kingdom, one must give everything. [Cf. Mt 13:44–45; 22:1–4.] Words are not enough; deeds are required. [Cf. Mt 21:28–32.] (546)

 Suppose Jesus were to use simple things from your life to tell a parable about God's kingdom. What things (geography, situation, people) from your life would be included in the parable? What lesson would Jesus want you to learn?

_____ _____

_____

_____

Learning from parables

Work with two or three other people to complete the following chart. Read one parable at a time. Try to figure out who Jesus was talking to (his audience) and what he was trying to say. Finally, decide what the parable says to young people today.

Parable	Jesus' Audience	Jesus' Message	Young People Now
Matthew 13:33 Title:			
Matthew 13:45–46 Title:			
Matthew 13:47–48 Title:			
Luke 15:8–10 Title:			
Luke 19:12–26 Title:			

If time permits, rewrite one of these parables using modern-day language and examples. Read or act out the parable for the class.

Country roads

Capernaum was Jesus' "headquarters" for the next two years. From there, he set out on a number of journeys. Once he traveled northwest into Syro-Phonecia. Another time he headed northeast up to Caesarea-Philippi. On several occasions, he went south to Jerusalem. Much of the time, he just traveled on short journeys to the countrysides near Capernaum. He usually walked; sometimes he rode in a fishing boat.

CHECK IT OUT!

Bands of robbers roamed Palestine in the time of Jesus, making travel by oneself dangerous. Most people traveled in groups.

At times, Jesus would spend whole days in the countryside or at the seashore teaching in a more organized way. The people would gather around and settle down. Jesus would stand or sit in their midst and teach them about prayer or about true love of their neighbor. Often, the disciples would come to Jesus after a day of teaching filled with questions about the meaning of what he had been saying. He would then give them "special lessons" after the people had gone home for the night.

If you were following Jesus around as one of his disciples, it wouldn't seem like there was any plan to Jesus' trips. Probably there wasn't. Jesus would often slip off and pray by himself late at night or early in the morning. It was as if he needed to "recharge his spiritual batteries" by spending time in the presence of God the Father. Then, enlivened and moved by the Spirit, he would start out on the road again, teaching and healing along the way.

Scripture Search

Match the following activities of Jesus with their passages in the Gospels:

_____ 1. Matthew 5:1–12   A. Jesus teaches a crowd at the seashore.

_____ 2. Luke 18:35–43   B. Jesus gives his disciples a "special lesson" at day's end.

_____ 3. Matthew 13:36–43   C. Jesus teaches a crowd from the hillside.

_____ 4. Mark 3:7–9   D. Jesus takes time to "recharge his spiritual batteries."

_____ 5. Mark 1:35   E. Jesus speaks to people along the roadside.

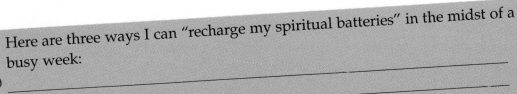

Here are three ways I can "recharge my spiritual batteries" in the midst of a busy week:

_____

_____

Here is one thing I am going to do today to spend time in the presence of God:

_____

More parables

Work with two or three other people to complete the following chart. Read one parable at a time. Try to figure out who Jesus was talking to (his audience) and what he was trying to say. Finally, decide what the parable says to young people today.

Parable	Jesus' Audience	Jesus' Message	Young People Now
Matthew 13:4–8, 18–23 Title:			
Matthew 13:24–30 Title:			
Matthew 13:44 Title:			
Luke 10:30–37 Title:			
Luke 15:4–7 Title:			

If time permits, rewrite one of these parables using modern-day language and examples.
Read or act out the parable for the class.

Our daily bread

In the Lord's Prayer, we ask God our Father to give us our daily bread. These words are both symbolic and literal. In one sense, we are praying that God will provide us with the physical things we need to live from day to day. These include bread (food), water, clothing, shelter, and money. In another sense, we are praying that God will fill us with what we need to live spiritually. Such things include a sense of God's presence and love, a sense of peace, and a sense of well-being.

As you have already learned, Jesus showed us that there is a vital connection between the physical world and the spiritual one. We find God in the ordinariness of our daily lives and relationships.

At first, people were enthusiastic about Jesus' message. But later some people began to have trouble with Jesus' teachings. They felt that Jesus was going too far with his talk about being the Bread of Life. "I am the bread of life. Whoever comes to me will never be hungry, and whoever believes in me will never be thirsty" (John 6:35).

Jesus' revolutionary message was indeed challenging to many people.

When many of his disciples heard it, they said, "This teaching is difficult; who can accept it?" But Jesus, being aware that his disciples were complaining about it, said to them, "Does this offend you? Then what if you were to see the Son of Man ascending to where he was before? It is the spirit that gives life; the flesh is useless. The words that I have spoken to you are spirit and life. But among you there are some who do not believe." For Jesus knew from the first who were the ones who did not believe, and who was the one that would betray him. And he said, "For this reason I have told you that no on can come to me unless it is granted by the Father."

Because of this many disciples turned back and no longer went about with him. So Jesus asked the twelve, "Do you also wish to go away?" Simon Peter answered him, "Lord, to whom can we go? You have the words of eternal life. We have come to believe and know that you are the Holy One of God." (John 6:60–69)

". . . if God so clothes the grass of the field, which is alive today and tomorrow is thrown into the oven, how much more will he clothe you—you of little faith! And do not keep striving for what you are to eat and what you are to drink, and do not keep worrying . . . your Father knows that you need them." (Luke 12:28–30)

Briefly discuss ways we can grow in our trust in Jesus as our daily bread, the Bread of Life.

This past week, Jesus has been the bread of my life in the following ways:

_____

_____

Jesus,

Help me be satisfied with simple things and help me always see you in my day-to-day life.

Help me persevere in humbly following you and Abba, your Father.

Help me never stray from the path of living in your kingdom and attaining life everlasting with you.

Amen.

Homework

Unscramble the words in the following Scripture passages (NAB). Be prepared to discuss the meaning of these passages at the next class meeting.

"Therefore I tell you, do not **ryorw** (1) _____ about your life and what you will eat, or about your body and what you will wear. For **feil** (2) _____ is more than food and the body more than **gholtcni** (3) _____ ." (Luke 12:22)

"If God so clothes the **sargs** (4) _____ in the field that grows today and is thrown into the oven **rwooortm** (5) _____ , will he not much more **vedopir**

(6) _____ for you, O you of little **atifh** (7) _____ ?" (Luke 12:28)

"My **ehrta** (8) _____ is moved with pity for the crowd, because they have been with me now for **eterh** (9) _____ days and have **tgnnhio** (10) _____ to eat." (Mark 8:2)

Then, taking the seven **vsolea** (11) _____ he gave thanks, broke them, and gave them to his **pcdlsseii** (12) _____ to distribute, and they distributed them to the **wordc** (13) _____ . (Mark 8:6)

When the **bhbaats** (14) _____ came he began to teach in the **auggyesno** (15) _____ , and many who heard him were astonished. (Mark 6:2)

"A **theropp** (16) _____ is not without **oohrn** (17) _____ except in his native place and **gonam** (18) _____ his own kin and in his own house." (Mark 6:4)

He was **zaadem** (19) _____ at their **kalc** (20) _____ of faith. (Mark 6:6)

6

Friends and Enemies

What others say

We can discover a lot about who a person is by the friends and enemies that person has. Who your friends are can give us a clue about what you like and dislike, what you value and find important. Who your enemies are can also tell us something about your character and what you stand for.

Who are three of your closest friends? List them here:

_____

_____

_____

Why are these people your friends?

_____

_____

_____

How do you think your friends see you? Who would they say you are?

_____

_____

_____

Think of someone you would consider to be your enemy. Why is this person your enemy?

_____

_____

How do you think this person sees you? How would he or she describe you to others?

_____

_____

_____

Who is the "real" you: the person described by friends or the person described by enemies? Explain your answer and try to give examples.

_____

_____

_____

_____

The friends of Jesus

We can learn something about who Jesus was by taking a closer look at who his friends, his followers, were. Actually, Jesus gained followers from every class of people in Jewish society. Some of his friends were wealthy and influential; others were religious leaders. Although Jesus challenged and sometimes criticized the wealthy and the religious leaders, he always welcomed them if they were sincerely interested in his message.

CHECK IT OUT!

Zacchaeus was one of the wealthy friends of Jesus (Luke 19:1–10). Nicodemus was a Jewish leader who became a follower of Jesus (John 3:1–21).

The large majority of Jesus' followers came from the working classes and from those who were poor—shopkeepers, farmhands, shepherds, fishermen, and servants. Jesus also drew his followers from the ranks of the public sinners, like prostitutes and tax collectors (also known as publicans) who were seen as traitors to the Jewish people because they worked for the Romans. Other social outcasts, such as lepers, Samaritans, and some of the Roman soldiers themselves, were attracted to Jesus and his message. In short, Jesus proclaimed his good news to everyone.

Women

Although Jewish men had deep respect for their wives and daughters and treated them well, women had no place in Jewish public life. They had no voice in politics and no role in religious rituals or services. In many cases, women were treated as possessions rather than as people. Their lives, their welfare, and their futures were, to a large extent, dependent on men.

Jesus, being revolutionary, treated women as equals. He publicly came to their defense. He praised their faith and their virtue and encouraged men to learn from them. He respected their opinion. His very first miracle, at Cana, was done at the request of a woman, his mother. Jesus talked freely with women in public. He welcomed them when they came to listen to him.

It's not surprising then, that some of Jesus' most courageous and faithful followers were women. When Jesus was crucified, his apostles fled and hid, but some of the women stayed with Jesus to the very end, standing by his cross. It was women who first discovered his resurrection and bore the news to his apostles.

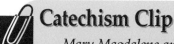

In a small group, read the following Scripture passages. For each passage, list the women involved. Write a short summary of each passage's story.

Matthew 26:6–13

Women:

Summary:

Luke 24:1–12

Women:

Summary:

Luke 8:1–3

Women:

Summary:

John 4:1–42

Women:

Summary:

Luke 10:38–42

Women:

Summary:

As a group, retell your Scripture passage for the class, using one of the following formats:

- Reading and pantomime
- Radio news broadcast
- Children's story
- TV talk show interview

Disciples

The people who changed their lives because of the good news of Jesus can be divided into two groups. The first (and largest) group **included people** who, after their conversion, returned to their home and to their work as before, but with a big difference. The seeds of a new faith had been planted in their hearts. They now **understood** that God was Abba and that God's kingdom was a realm of peace, humility, and justice. They may not have looked any different when they returned home, but, in fact, they now viewed the world differently.

People in the second group of followers actually left their homes, their jobs, and their **families** after they came to believe in Jesus. They followed him more or less full-time, becoming his disciples (students). They sought to hear and to understand every word he said. They were available and eager to help in any way they could. Most disciples were men, but some women followed Jesus full-time, too.

It's hard to say for sure how many disciples Jesus had. The Gospels make reference at one point to seventy-two (Luke 10:1). Jesus gave special attention to his disciples. He taught and explained things to them that he didn't always share with the crowds. He trained them to proclaim his message and sent them on training missions. To make their work easier he shared with them the power he had received from the Father to heal and cast out demons. This band of full-time disciples was to become the beginnings of the Church. Through these followers, Jesus inaugurated the kingdom of God here on earth. The Church is the seed and beginning of this kingdom.

After this the Lord appointed seventy others and sent them on ahead of him in pairs to every town and place where he himself intended to go. (Luke 10:1)

CHECK IT OUT!

After Judas' betrayal and death, the apostles chose Matthias to replace him. Matthias had been one of Jesus' full-time disciples from almost the beginning of his ministry (Acts 1:15–26).

Looking for Answers!

Check the correct reference.

The day on which the Holy Spirit descended on Jesus' disciples was:

____ a. Acts 13:4

____ b. Hebrews 10:19–22

____ c. 2 John 4

____ d. Acts 2:1

Answer: _____

Discuss these questions in class:

1. What is something positive you have learned from a friend? In what way has your life (thoughts, attitudes, behavior, feelings) changed because of a friend?

2. What is something positive you have learned from a TV or radio personality? In what way has your life (thoughts, attitudes, behavior, feelings) changed as a result of seeing or hearing this person?

3. Why do you think most people who followed Jesus chose to return to their families and jobs? What were the advantages? How do you think their daily lives and relationships changed as a result of being friends with Jesus?

4. Why do you think some people left everything to follow Jesus as he traveled around Palestine? What were the advantages? How do you think their daily lives and relationships changed as a result of being friends with Jesus?

5. Do you think one group of people was "better" or "holier" than the other? Explain.

If I were a follower of Jesus 2000 years, ago, which group would I belong to? Would I follow Jesus in the context of my own home and job? Or would I become a full-time disciple?

This is my choice: _____

Here are three reasons for my choice:

1. _____

2. _____

3. _____

Looking for Answers!

Check the correct reference.

The first disciple to be martyred for his faith in Jesus was:

____ a. Acts 2:42–47

____ b. Acts 7:54–60

____ c. Acts 16:25–34

____ d. Acts 28:30–31

Answer: _____

Apostles

Jesus personally chose twelve of his full-time disciples to be his closest companions and friends. We now call these twelve the *apostles*. They traveled and lived together with Jesus, sharing everything in common for almost three years.

Jesus trained the apostles to be the foundation of his Church, the ones chosen to carry his name and his message to the whole world. And yet they were quite ordinary men in just about every area, even holiness. Most of them didn't have any special education or any special skills beyond what they had developed at their work. All but one apostle turned coward at the end and hid after Jesus was arrested. One apostle even betrayed him.

We don't know much about the apostles or why Jesus chose them. But here is a little of what we do know:

- Eleven of the twelve were from Galilee, Jesus' own area. Judas was possibly from Carioth, a town in Judea in southern Palestine. Three apostles (James the Less, Jude, and Simon the Zealot) were related to Jesus, probably as cousins.
- Peter, Andrew, James, John, and Philip were fishermen. Matthew (also called Levi) was a tax collector. There were three sets of brothers: Peter and Andrew, James and John, James the Less and Simon the Zealot.
- The names of two apostles, John and Matthew, are associated with Gospels.
- Thomas was a questioner and doubter.
- Philip didn't seem to understand what Jesus was about.
- John and James had bad tempers, so much so that Jesus nicknamed them "the sons of thunder."
- Jesus appointed Peter the leader of the apostles and almost immediately afterwards had to correct him for his faulty thinking.
- Judas betrayed Jesus for thirty pieces of silver.

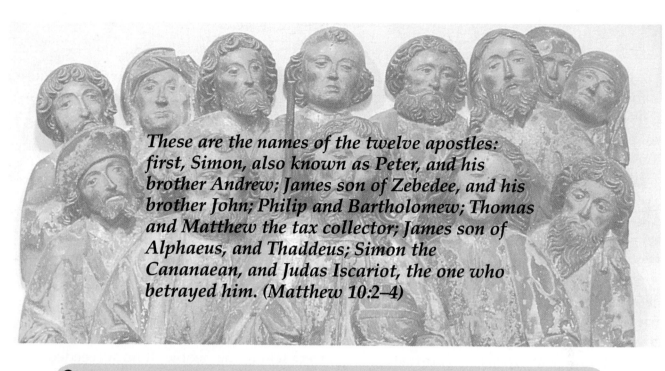

These are the names of the twelve apostles: first, Simon, also known as Peter, and his brother Andrew; James son of Zebedee, and his brother John; Philip and Bartholomew; Thomas and Matthew the tax collector; James son of Alphaeus, and Thaddeus; Simon the Cananaean, and Judas Iscariot, the one who betrayed him. (Matthew 10:2–4)

 ## Catechism Clip

From the beginning of his public life, Jesus chose certain men, twelve in number, to be with him and to participate in his mission. [Cf. Mk 3:13–19.] He gives the Twelve a share in his authority and "sent them out to preach the kingdom of God and to heal." [Lk 9:2.] (551)

Activity

Using a variety of research resources, list below how and when it is thought that each of the twelve apostles died.

- Simon Peter
- Andrew
- James, Zebedee's son
- John, Zebedee's son
- Philip
- Batholomew
- Thomas
- Matthew the tax collector
- James, son of Alphaeus
- Thaddaeus
- Simon the Zealot Party member
- Judas Iscariot

The enemies of Jesus

Most of Jesus' enemies came from the following groups of religious leaders.

Pharisees. The Pharisees—mostly laymen, not priests—were religious reformers. They stressed morality as the strictest kind of obedience to the Law. They were hard judges of anyone who didn't follow the Law strictly. Although the Pharisees had the reputation of being holy, Jesus considered some of them hypocrites.

Sadducees. The Sadducees tended to be the wealthy, ruling class of Jewish society. They controlled the Sanhedrin, a senate that governed the Jewish people. A big reason they opposed Jesus was their fear that a political revolt would cause the Roman army to come down hard on them.

Scribes. Scribes, members of the educated and scholarly class, devoted their lives to studying and preserving the Scriptures. The people usually looked to the scribes for the correct interpretation of the Scriptures and of all religious matters. The interpretation of the scribes often differed from what Jesus taught.

Priests. In the Jewish religion, a priest was a man born into the priestly family that descended from Levi. Priests took turns serving in the Temple. They were an elite group and had special privileges. Dishonest ones could become wealthy by overcharging for their services and by using the Temple offerings for their own purposes. For this reason, some priests feared and opposed Jesus.

We can't really judge these religious leaders. Many of them had good intentions. Some of them sincerely felt that Jesus was a false prophet who was leading innocent people away from true belief in God and the covenant. They just didn't believe that Jesus was the Messiah of God. They thought his teaching was a corruption of the Law.

Some religious leaders who opposed Jesus were caught up in the idea of their own importance. They enjoyed the power and respect that people gave them. They strayed from the real meaning of the covenant and lived by external rules and observances that allowed them to be selfish and still think they were holy. They considered their wealth proof of God's approval of them. They felt that people who were poor were sinners and their poverty was a punishment from God.

No wonder such leaders saw Jesus as their mortal enemy. What he taught was often in direct contradiction to what they were telling the people. If he succeeded in converting the people to his way of thinking, their whole world would crumble. They'd lose everything—reputation, power, and wealth.

Today's world

Jesus has his enemies today, also. Maybe they don't belong to an organized group, like the Pharisees or Sadducees, but, in their own way, they try to draw people away from Jesus. They ridicule and laugh at the people who take Jesus seriously. They are afraid that if Jesus' message becomes too popular, they'll lose the wealth and power they now possess. So they actively promote the false values they live by.

Jesus and you

If we judge on the surface, Jesus seems to have chosen a weak group to be the foundation of his Church. But it is now 2000 years later, and the Church is still going strong. Apparently, Jesus knew what he was doing.

And he knows what he is doing **today** when he chooses you to be one of his **followers**. Under your weaknesses and **inexperience**, Jesus can see the potential, the **heart**, of a true disciple.

What do you think are some indications that a person is a disciple of Jesus today?
_____
Would you qualify? Why or why not?
_____
_____

Just then a lawyer stood up to test Jesus. "Teacher," he said, "What must I do to inherit eternal life?" . . . He answered, "You shall love the Lord your God with all your heart, and with all your soul, and with all your strength, and with all your mind; and your neighbor as yourself." (Luke 10:25–27)

Briefly discuss whether you think Jesus expects the same kind of dedication to him from followers your age as he does from older people. Why or why not?

What is Jesus asking me to do right now in terms of following him?
_____
_____
_____

Jesus,

Help me recognize that every person is a valued, unique individual in the eyes of God and should be treated with respect.

Help me rid myself of prejudices and discriminatory behavior.

Help me always recognize that I have a responsibility to care for and help others.

Amen.

Homework

Complete the following crossword puzzle by filling in the blanks.

Followers of Jesus

Jesus welcomed anyone (27 across) interested in his message. Jesus' followers came from every class of Jewish (1 across). Many of them were (7 down). Some of Jesus' followers had been (16 across) sinners. Others, whom the Jewish people called (34 across), worked for the Romans. Jesus (14 across) his good news to everyone. Jesus treated (5 across) as equals. Jesus worked his first miracle for a woman at (2 down). Some women stayed with Jesus to the end, standing by his (9 across).

The (24 down) of faith were planted in many people who heard Jesus preach. Jesus talked about God as (17 across). The kingdom of God is one of (28 across), humility, and justice.

Some hearers became (4 down), or students, of Jesus. Jesus trained some of his followers to proclaim his (18 down). Jesus' disciples were the beginnings of the (9 down). Even today, Jesus can see the potential, the (15 across), of a true disciple.

The Apostles

Some of Jesus' closest followers were called (12 across). They and Jesus shared everything in (10 across). There were (23 down) apostles. They were quite (11 down) people. Matthew was a (22 across) collector. (20 down) betrayed Jesus. Simon was a (38 across). James the (32 down) was probably related to Jesus. One of the (37 across) is attributed to John. (25 across) was the brother of Peter. (29 down) was the brother of James the Less. (20 across) and James had bad tempers. (8 down) was a doubter. (36 down) was the brother of Andrew. (34 down) didn't seem to understand Jesus. Some of the apostles were (40 across). Jesus called John and James "(39 across) of thunder."

Enemies of Jesus

Some of Jesus' enemies were religious (3 across). The (13 down) were religious reformers. The (21 across) controlled the Sanhedrin. (35 across) devoted their lives to studying and preserving the Scriptures. Priests belonged to the family of (26 down). Some of these people thought Jesus was a (19 down) prophet. Some did not want to believe that Jesus was the (6 down). Others thought that Jesus' teachings corrupted the (30 down). Some thought that wealth was (33 down) of God's approval. Like today, some people promoted false (31 across).

Don't Forget!

A different view

Who we are today is not necessarily what we will remember about ourselves in the future. Likewise, who other people see us as today is not necessarily what people will remember about us a year from now.

The passing of time gives us a different view. We remember some things, and we forget others. What do you remember about yourself when you were:

Four?_____

_____

Seven?_____

_____

Ten?_____

_____

What do you remember about your parent(s)/guardian(s) when you were:

Four?_____

_____

Seven?_____

_____

Ten?_____

_____

In two years, what would you like other people to remember about who you are right now?

_____

_____

Describe yourself (how you look, your feelings, your worries, your dreams) right now. Write down some things about yourself that you don't want to forget.

_____

_____

_____

The other side of Jesus

Up to now, we've talked mainly about the human side of Jesus. Now it's time to explore another side of who Jesus is: his divinity, or identity as the Son of God.

In Jesus we encounter a most profound mystery. Two natures, one fully divine, the other fully human, are united in the one divine Person, Jesus, the son of Mary and the eternal Son of God the Father. Paul said, "Jesus is like us in all things except sin" and thus experienced the kinds of human joys, struggles, and disappointments common to all of us. Jesus is at the same time the divine Son of God. And it is precisely our belief in Jesus' divinity that is the foundation for all the core beliefs we hold as his disciples; he is the source of all truth; he is the Savior of the world; he sits now at the Father's right hand to plead for us. The challenge for us as disciples of Jesus is to maintain at all times that careful balance our belief in the mystery of the incarnation demands. Jesus is fully human and fully divine.

Jesus knew the Scriptures very well. He knew that most Jews had only a partial understanding of what the Messiah would be like. But Jesus knew that the Messiah would serve God's people through suffering. So Jesus knew that he would suffer and someday be put to death. Even though the Scriptures also revealed that God would raise the Messiah from the dead, Jesus had to go about his ministry with the painful knowledge that his days were numbered.

1. Would you want to know everything that will happen to you in the future? Why or why not?
2. When do you think you will know everything there is to know about yourself?

CHECK IT OUT!

Incarnation is the belief that for the salvation of the world, the Son of God, while remaining fully divine, became truly and fully human (see John 1:14).

Looking Ahead

Knowing that his time here on earth was limited, Jesus began to organize and train his followers. He needed them to continue his ministry after his death. In short, Jesus began to establish his Church.

Calling apostles and disciples was one step in this process. Giving them special instructions apart from the crowds was another step in establishing the Church. Sending them on training missions and sharing his powers with them was yet another step. Basically, Jesus prepared his apostles and other disciples for three key roles—the main aspects of his own mission.

Prophets

First, Jesus prepared his apostles and disciples to be prophets like himself. They would have the task of teaching the good news about God and proclaiming God's kingdom.

CHECK IT OUT!

The word *prophet* comes from the Greek word meaning "to speak out." Only indirectly does it mean to foretell the future. Not all prophets foretell the future, but they all speak out against injustice and a lack of holiness.

Priests

Second, the apostles and disciples were to continue Jesus' priestly role. A priest, in this sense, is someone who acts as a bridge between God and people. Through the priest (who represents Jesus), God blesses and forgives people. Through the priest (who again represents Jesus), people offer their prayers, praise, and thanks to God.

CHECK IT OUT!

Melchizedek is the first priest mentioned in the Old Testament to offer a sacrifice of bread and wine to God. He is a model and prefigurement of all our ordained priests today.

Servant-Kings

Finally, Jesus trained his followers to be shepherds or servants. As Messiah, Jesus was King David's heir. He had the right to a kingly title and kingly authority. But Jesus' idea of Messiah also incorporated the idea of suffering servant. Jesus taught that the strong and the powerful should be the servants of those who are poor and weak. To be king of all, in Jesus' scheme of things, is to be servant of all.

So Jesus demanded that those who were to have authority in his Church when he was gone must be the servants of the people. They should regard themselves as gentle, caring, protective shepherds like Jesus, who called himself the Good Shepherd. Jesus really had to struggle to get this idea across to his apostles. Remember, most of them were ambitious men who were only too eager to get into positions of honor and power.

Catechism Clip

Jesus fulfilled the messianic hope of Israel in his threefold office of priest, prophet, and king. (436)

God the Father sent Jesus to be a prophet, priest, and servant-king of the people. Knowing this mission would have to be carried on after he was gone, he carefully prepared his apostles and other disciples for the task. Two thousand years later, the Church and all of us in it, as disciples of Jesus, are expected to continue that same mission. Each of us is called to participate in Jesus' prophetic, priestly, and servant mission.

CHECK IT OUT!

Our own Baptism gives each of us a personal share in Jesus' threefold mission as priest, prophet, and servant-king.

Read the following Scripture passages. Write down what you know about Jesus—how he carried out this mission in his own ministry. Then write down how Jesus calls you, his follower, to continue this mission today. Give one specific example, if possible.

Mission	Scripture	Jesus	You
Prophet	Isaiah 61:1–2		
Priest	Hebrews 5:1–10		
Servant-King	John 13:1–17		

Seven ways to remember Jesus

Basically, Jesus instructed his apostles and other disciples to be like him, to imitate him. From Jesus' actions, they learned what he valued. For example, they observed the special concern Jesus had for those who were sick. They also saw that Jesus spent much time with sinners—calling them to conversion, offering them forgiveness, and giving them a fresh start.

So, after his resurrection when Jesus told his apostles to go out in the world and baptize, they knew, in general, what they were supposed to do. They had watched Jesus many times lead people to conversion and to new faith in God. When he instructed them to forgive sin in his name, they had a pretty good idea of what that meant, too. Gradually, the apostles and those who came after them organized the main aspects of Jesus' ministry into what we now call the seven sacraments. The sacraments are rooted in the words and actions of Jesus. That's why we say they were *instituted by Jesus*. They are actual continuations, under the signs and words used by the Church, of Jesus' own actions. In the sacraments, Jesus is present—healing, forgiving, and uniting us with God and each other.

Fill in the following chart. Then discuss, in class, how each sacrament continues Jesus' ministry today.

The Seven Sacraments

Sacraments of Initiation (Belonging)

_____

_____

_____

Sacraments of Healing

_____

_____

Sacraments of Vocation and Service

_____

_____

Remember me

When people are near death, they often leave a last will or special remembrance by which their loved ones can remember them. It was no different for Jesus. When Jesus traveled to Jerusalem with his disciples, he knew his death was near. He chose a last meal as the opportunity to give his disciples a final memorial of himself. The meal happened to be the annual Jewish Passover meal.

CHECK IT OUT!

The Jewish people still celebrate the Passover meal each spring to recall their covenant with God who saved them from the Egyptians. This meal is also called the *Seder* meal.

Many times during his teaching, Jesus used the image of a meal or a banquet to describe God's kingdom. In many ways, a meal sums up everything Jesus taught. At a meal, the main idea is to share. We pass the food around. We encourage others to take the bigger portion (at least we should). We respect one another's human dignity by using good manners. Most people use the meal as a time to pray and to recall God's goodness and blessings.

Jesus did several special things at his last Passover meal. He began by washing the feet of all the apostles. Jesus assumed the role of the lowest of servants or of a slave. Afterward he made it clear that, as a memorial to him, he wanted his apostles to act the same way. If they were willing to assume the role of the lowest of servants in the care and concern they showed for others, they would be keeping Jesus' memory alive.

CHECK IT OUT!

It was a custom in those days to provide guests with water and towels to wash their feet when they arrived. Streets were dusty. People wore sandals. Often it was hot. To wash one's feet on arrival was both refreshing and a courtesy.

During much of the supper, Jesus talked in a deeper way than he had ever shared before. He was sad and troubled, but his deep love for his apostles was also obvious. Jesus talked about his special relationship with God. He talked about heaven and the special places the apostles would have in it. And he talked about the fact that one of them was going to betray him.

While they were eating, Jesus took a loaf of bread, and after blessing it, gave it to the disciples, and said, "Take, eat, this is my body." Then he took a cup, and after giving thanks he gave it to them, saying, "Drink from it, all of you; for this is my blood of the covenant, which is poured out for many for the forgiveness of sins." (Matthew 26:26–28)

When all had eaten the bread and drunk the wine, Jesus instructed them very clearly. "Do this in memory of me."

If I knew I was going to die tomorrow, here are the gifts I'd want to leave my family and friends to help them remember me:

_____

_____

_____

_____

_____

Looking for Answers!

Check the correct reference.

At the Last Supper the apostle who swore he would never leave Jesus was:

_____ a. Matthew 26:14–16

_____ b. Mark 15:16–20

_____ c. Luke 22:66–71

_____ d. John 13:36–38

Answer: _____

81

A sacrifice and a memorial meal

It was only after Jesus' death and resurrection that the apostles began to understand what Jesus meant at the Last Supper. That memorial meal was to recall not only all that Jesus did and taught during his life, but also his death on the cross and his resurrection from death. It was to recall the fact that Jesus sacrificed himself to save them and all people.

Today, we call this memorial meal the Holy Sacrifice of the Mass or the Eucharistic Meal. The Mass is both a sacrifice and a meal. Above all, it is the Church gathering, as Jesus asked, to remember all he said and did. At the Mass, we remember how Jesus died for us and was raised from death for us. We remember how we are to share our lives and our goods with others and how we are to be servants to one another.

With the words of consecration in the Eucharistic Prayer, Jesus himself becomes truly present in our midst. He is just as present today as he was at the table with the apostles at the first Eucharist. Jesus is present under the signs of the bread and wine that we offer to God as a sacrifice in union with Jesus' own suffering and death. Jesus is present when we share Communion, Christ's sacramental Body and Blood, with each other.

By gathering to celebrate the Eucharist, we enable Jesus to live in each of us and to continue his ministry through us. We go out from each Eucharist with a specific mission—to bring Jesus into our homes, our neighborhoods, and our schools. Jesus lives in the Church, in the sacraments, and in us!

CHECK IT OUT!

Eucharist is a Greek word meaning "thanksgiving." The Mass is a sacrifice-meal that offers thanks to God for giving us salvation through Jesus.

Activity

Referring to Eucharistic Prayer IV (pages 103–104 of the appendix), answer the following questions:

1. What do we acknowledge about the Father?

2. What has been offered again and again to humanity?

3. Whom did the Father send to be our Savior?

4. Jesus is like humans in everything but what?

5. What did Jesus proclaim to those who were poor? To those who were imprisoned? To those who were sorrowing?

6. How did Jesus destroy death and restore life?

7. What was the first gift sent to those who believe?

8. What offerings become the Body and Blood of Jesus Christ our Lord?

Order of the Mass

Work as a team with one other person to complete the following outline of the Mass. Use a missalette, if needed. Be prepared to discuss what happens at each part of the Mass.

Acclamation

Antiphon

Blessing

Bread

Communion

Concluding

Dialogue

Dismissal

Eucharist

Eucharistic

Eucharistic Prayer

Faith

First reading

Gifts

Gospel

Great Amen

Homily

Intercessions

Lord's

Memorial

Peace

Penitential rite

Prayer

Prayer after Communion

Prayer over the gifts

Preface

Psalm

Rite

Second reading

Silent

Word

I. Introductory Rites
    A. Entrance _____
    B. Greeting
    C. _____
    D. Lord, Have Mercy
    E. Gloria
    F. Opening _____

II. Liturgy of the _____
    A. _____
    B. Responsorial _____
    C. _____
    D. Gospel _____
    E. _____
    F. _____
    G. Profession of _____
    H. Intercessions _____

III. Liturgy of the _____
    A. Preparation of the _____
    B. _____
    C. _____ Prayer
        1. Introductory _____
        2. _____
        3. _____ I, II, III, or IV
        4. _____ Acclamation
        5. _____
    D. Communion _____
        1. The _____ Prayer
        2. Sign of _____
        3. Breaking of the _____
        4. _____
        5. Communion Antiphon
        6. _____ prayer
        7. _____

IV. _____ Rite
    A. _____
    B. _____

The Mass and sacraments today

As you have learned, the Eucharist and the other sacraments have their origins in the ministry of Jesus. But the Mass and sacraments as we celebrate them today have gone through centuries of development. Certain core parts, or essentials, have always been present. The Eucharistic celebration always includes the proclamation of the word, thanks and praise to God the Father, the consecration of bread and wine, and the reception of the Lord's Body and Blood.

But other parts (particular words or actions or prayers) may have changed. For example, over the centuries, the Church has celebrated the Eucharistic meal in many different ways. These ways include such things as the language used, the kinds of vestments the priest was expected to wear, various prayers and hymns, the gestures and symbols used (for example, the sign of peace, candles, and incense).

These external differences usually came from the customs of the time, which people felt were appropriate. For example, for a long time women were expected to wear hats or veils to Mass. There was even a time when the organ was outlawed for Church use because it was considered an instrument of secular music.

Despite these changes, the core of the Mass and the sacraments has always remained the same. Jesus becomes present through the changing of the bread and wine into the Body and Blood of Christ during the consecration of the Mass. We remember and celebrate Jesus' words and actions. Through the power of the Holy Spirit, we receive the grace we need to continue Jesus' mission in the world today.

CHECK IT OUT!

For a long time, in the West, the Mass and sacraments were celebrated in Latin only. Latin remained the "official" language of liturgy even when times changed and people no longer understood it. It was not until the Second Vatican Council in the 1960s that liturgies in the Western or Roman Rite were once more celebrated in the vernacular language (the language of the people present).

Catechism Clip

The seven sacraments touch all the stages and all the important moments of Christian life [Cf. St. Thomas Aquinas, STh III, 6, 5, 1]: they give birth and increase, healing and mission to the Christian's life of faith. There is thus a certain resemblance between the stages of natural life and the stages of the spiritual life. (1210)

- How do you really feel about the Mass? Is it something you can get excited about? Why or why not?

_____

_____

- What are some steps you could take to help make the Mass more of an experience of Jesus' presence?

_____

_____

- How do you think Jesus plans to be present in today's society through people like you?

_____

_____

Work with your classmates to create a mural that shows the seven sacraments. Divide the mural into seven sections. Choose one sacrament to illustrate in each section. Draw a picture of the celebration or use words and/or symbols to illustrate the sacrament. Try to show how we remember Jesus and continue his ministry through this sacrament. When you have finished, discuss your portion of the mural. Then hang the mural in a place where everyone can see it.

Reflection

"A dispute also arose among them as to which one of them was to be regarded as the greatest." But [Jesus] said to them, "Let the greatest among you become like the youngest, and the leader like one who serves." (Luke 22:24–26)

Briefly discuss how we can serve others today as Jesus did.

One way I will act as a prophet of good news this week:

_____

One way I will act as a priest (bring people closer to God) this week:

_____

One way I will act as a servant to others this week:

_____

Jesus,

Help me never forget you or your words or your ministry. Give me the desire to know you better through your words in Scripture.

Help me celebrate the Eucharist and other sacraments often and reflect on their meaning.

Help me be grateful that I have been called to be a Christian and remember that you are with me always.

Amen.

Homewonk

Match the words in Column A with their description in Column B. Perhaps ask a parent or older brother or sister to help you. Be prepared to discuss the answers in class.

A

_____ 1. bread and wine

_____ 2. incense

_____ 3. candles

_____ 4. vestments

_____ 5. alb

_____ 6. sign of peace

_____ 7. paten

_____ 8. chasuble

_____ 9. cruets

_____ 10. stole

_____ 11. Seder

_____ 12. host

_____ 13. altar cloth

_____ 14. chalice

_____ 15. lectionary

B

A. long, narrow vestment worn around the neck or across the left shoulder

B. placed near or on the altar

C. book with readings for Mass

D. long white robe worn by the priest at Mass

E. exchange of greetings before Communion

F. special cup used at Mass

G. the Jewish Passover meal

H. table covering at Mass

I. plate used for host at Mass

J. become Jesus' Body and Blood

K. hold water and wine

L. large outer garment worn by priest at Mass

M. the bread used at Mass

N. sweet-smelling smoke

O. the garments the priest wears at Mass

8

Who Do You Say That I Am?

Unanswered questions

Throughout this course, we've been trying to discover just who Jesus is. We've talked about his human life, his message about God's kingdom, his miracles, and his divinity. But, if you're like most people, you've probably still got some unanswered questions about Jesus. For example, if Jesus is really the Son of God, why did he have to suffer and die on the cross in order to redeem us? Why didn't he just give a command, and we would be saved?

Human suffering and death are great mysteries. People of all centuries find it hard to understand why bad things happen to good people. If God is good, why is there so much suffering in the world? The fact that God permits physical and moral evil is illustrated by Jesus' death. Faith assures us that God would not permit an evil if a good did not come from that evil.

To understand who Jesus really is, we need to tackle these questions. We need to take a closer look at his suffering and death. We have to see what they meant to him and what they mean for us.

1. What are some types of suffering present in the world today?

2. Why do you think bad things sometimes happen to good people?

3. If God is good, why is there so much suffering in the world?

4. Why do you think Jesus chose to suffer and die in order to redeem us? Why didn't he choose some other way?

Describe some pain you or a family member experienced in the past year:

_____

_____

Did anything good come from the experience? If so, what?

_____

_____

Jesus' passion and death

Crucifixion is one of the cruelest, most painful kinds of torture humankind has ever invented. Jesus' suffering was real, and it was extreme. But we shouldn't get too distracted by how much suffering Jesus endured in his last hours. Many people have suffered longer and possibly more painful forms of death. Tales from the Nazi death camps of World War II are proof of that.

The real question is why Jesus suffered at all. To be honest, the answer is still a mystery. But we can begin to answer the question. Jesus' suffering and death was his supreme act of trust in and obedience to God. In anyone's eyes (especially in Jesus' eyes), his death seemed like the end, as if he had lived for nothing. But it was clear to Jesus that God wanted him to surrender to his enemies and allow them to kill him. Somehow, in some way, God would turn this apparent defeat into victory and success. That's what Jesus believed to his dying breath. And that's why Jesus obeyed his Father's will, no matter how much suffering it caused him.

Trust and obedience were the two attitudes that humans had failed to show toward God from their very creation onward. They trusted in their own power. They did whatever they wanted. Jesus turned all that around. In his own person, he made a perfect act of trust in and obedience to God in the name of all of us and for the benefit of all of us.

The salvation Jesus won for us on the cross isn't measured in terms of how much physical pain he suffered. It is measured in how completely he continued to trust and obey God his Father, regardless of the pain and failure he experienced. No one else had ever trusted God so completely or obeyed God so perfectly.

Again he went away for the second time and prayed, "My Father, if this cannot pass unless I drink it, your will be done." (Matthew 26:42)

Trust and obedience

Review the final hours of Jesus' life by working with a partner to put the following events in order. Then discuss in class how each event shows Jesus' complete trust in and obedience to God. If needed, consult these Scripture readings: Matthew 26:36–28:10, Mark 14:32–16:8; Luke 22:39–24:12.

____ Pilate had Jesus scourged in hopes that it would satisfy the Jewish leaders. It didn't. Finally, Pilate gave in to political pressure and agreed to have Jesus crucified.

____ Judas came to the garden with Temple guards who arrested Jesus. The apostles ran off.

____ The religious leaders placed a large stone over the entrance to the tomb and placed a guard there to make sure no one would come and take the body.

____ After the Last Supper, Jesus and his apostles went to a garden called Gethsemane. Jesus agonized in prayer over the decision to remain obedient to his Father and to allow himself to be crucified. Ultimately, he said "Yes" to God. Meanwhile his apostles fell asleep.

____ Jesus was taken to Pilate, the Roman governor. Pilate, trying to avoid trouble, sent Jesus to Herod, the Jewish ruler at that time. Herod sent him back to Pilate.

____ After about three hours on the cross, Jesus died. Two other criminals were crucified with him.

____ The priests and religious leaders held a secret, unofficial trial. Eventually, they agreed that Jesus was guilty of blasphemy because he refused to deny that he was the Son of God.

____ Some followers of Jesus, mostly women, got permission to take Jesus' body down and bury it. After some quick burial preparations, they laid his body in a borrowed, cave-like tomb.

____ Jesus was led out to a hill called Golgatha. He was stripped naked, nailed to the cross, and left to die.

____ On the third day, Jesus reappeared, alive, resurrected, transformed!

____ The priests and religious leaders held a quick, "official" trial and condemned Jesus for blasphemy, a crime punishable by death in Jewish law.

CHECK IT OUT!

The fourteen Stations of the Cross are a traditional Catholic devotion. They recount the final hours of Jesus' life.

Other Lessons

There are other lessons we can learn from the cross of Jesus. For one thing, it reveals to us just how real, cruel, and totally destructive evil actually is. Ultimately, evil wants to hate and destroy everything, even God. Left to itself, that's what it will always do, no matter how innocent and charming a mask evil can present when tempting us. The cross of Jesus unmasks evil and shows it to the world for what it really is.

Another lesson of the cross is the power of good. No matter how powerful evil can seem at times and no matter how complete the destruction it brings about, God remains in charge. God can undo the bad and restore the good. God can redeem and re-create, provided we trust in him and seek to obey him.

Finally, a lesson of the cross is the lesson of love, the love of God the Father who allowed his Son to die on the cross in order to reconcile us with himself. It's also the love of the Son who offered his life to his Father through the Holy Spirit to gain forgiveness for our sins.

So, whenever it seems as if evil is conquering all or that all is lost, we need only to gaze upon the crucifix. The trust and obedience Jesus shows us while hanging there can recall for us that God ultimately remains in charge. God always brings life out of death and victory out of defeat.

CHECK IT OUT!

Evil is personified in the New Testament by such names as Satan, the Prince of Darkness, Beelzebub, the Father of Lies, and the Prince of This World.

Evil and death are sometimes portrayed as darkness, winter, the ebb of the tide, a new moon, hunger, coldness, and so on. Goodness and life are sometimes portrayed as light, summer, the flow of the tide, a full moon, a banquet, warmth, and so on. Express what the cross of Jesus means to you in some creative way (song, poem, collage, drawing, banner, slide show, and so on) that shows the victory of good over evil.

Think about it

The cross of Jesus not only reveals something about who Jesus is. It also reveals who God is. Consider this: Jesus the Nazarene really is God-Man, fully divine as well as fully human. This means, in a sense, that God was born in a cave near Bethlehem. God grew up in a town called Nazareth. God did manual work as a carpenter. God washed the feet of the apostles. God felt hungry, cold, thirsty, and tired, just as we do. God became frustrated at times and angry. God laughed. God cried. God experienced the joy of having close friends. God experienced the pain of being lonely, laughed at, rejected, and betrayed. God was afraid. God loved us so much that God died by inches, nailed to a tree.

If we really think about it, it's very difficult to say that God is "too distant" or that God is "too important and too busy" to get involved in our concerns. It becomes impossible to believe that God can't really understand how we feel when we're lonely, laughed at by others, or afraid of what's going to happen. Because of the cross of Jesus, because of the suffering and death he freely chose, we can know for sure what a wonderful God we have.

Or think about this: Human nature must be wonderful and good if God freely chose to become human with us. Was human nature wounded and afflicted by sin? You bet. Was human nature in need of redemption and restoration? Definitely! But that didn't turn God away from us. God jumped right in, taking the bad with the good, in order to be with us and to restore us to our rightful dignity.

Remember these things when you begin to doubt your personal worth or importance as a human. God freely chose to be human with you and like you. If Jesus the Nazarene is God, what wonderful people we humans are!

Catechism Clip

It is love "to the end" [Jn 13:1] that confers on Christ's sacrifice its value as redemption and reparation, as atonement and satisfaction. He knew and loved us all when he offered his life. [Cf. Gal 2:20; Eph 5:2, 25.] (616)

More Food for Thought

Because we believe that Jesus the Nazarene is the Son of God, every word he ever said takes on a deep meaning for us. Every act and every gesture of Jesus is an act of God. No wonder the New Testament, our record of the words and deeds of Jesus, is so important for us Christians. Can God's words and deeds ever be unimportant or boring? Can we ever say "I know all that" when it comes to learning about what God said and did?

Because we believe that Jesus is the Son of God, the community he formed is no ordinary community. The Church that grew out of that first community of apostles and other disciples is no ordinary Church. It's God's Church, and it's the official way God wants to continue the mission Jesus began 2000 years ago in Galilee.

The same is true for the sacraments. God instituted them as special ways to be with us and to minister to us. Thus, can we ever say they are unimportant or unnecessary? If that's how we sometimes feel about them, we'd better think about it some more.

CHECK IT OUT!

The New Testament, which contains the words and deeds of Jesus and the teachings that flow from them, consists of the following books: four Gospels (Matthew, Mark, Luke, and John), the Acts of the Apostles, the Book of Revelation, and twenty-one letters. That's twenty-seven books in all.

94

Scripture Search

There are twenty-one *letters* (or *epistles*) in the New Testament. These writings were not placed in chronological order. Letters written by Paul are placed first, and his letters to communities are placed before those to individuals. Letters attributed to the same author, such as 1 Peter and 2 Peter, are kept together. Most of the letters follow a set pattern. First comes a greeting, naming the writer of the letter and for whom the letter is written. Next comes a prayer. Then the main body of the letter, usually answering questions or giving directions for moral Christian behavior. The letter concludes with greetings to certain individuals or churches, a closing prayer, and a farewell.

A familiarity with the letters in the New Testament is important as you grow in faith. At most Sunday liturgies the second reading comes from one of the letters. In small groups, work to complete the chart below.

	Author	Recipient of the letter	One teaching within the letter (cite source in the first column)
Romans ___ : ___			
1 Corinthians ___ : ___			
2 Corinthians ___ : ___			
Galatians ___ : ___			
Ephesians ___ : ___			
Philippians ___ : ___			
Colossians ___ : ___			
1 Thessalonians ___ : ___			
2 Thessalonians ___ : ___			
1 Timothy ___ : ___			
2 Timothy ___ : ___			
Titus ___ : ___			
Philemon ___ : ___			
Hebrews ___ : ___			
James ___ : ___			
1 Peter ___ : ___			
2 Peter ___ : ___			
1 John ___ : ___			
2 John ___ : ___			
3 John ___ : ___			
Jude ___ : ___			

What are your present feelings or beliefs about the Church? Why?

_____

_____

What are your present feelings or beliefs about the sacraments? Why?

_____

_____

At the Crossroads

Jesus once asked his disciples directly, "Who do you say that I am?" He's asking you much the same thing now at this crossroads in your life between childhood and adulthood.

Who do YOU say that Jesus is?

In this course, we've tried to rediscover some qualities of the "real" Jesus who preached in the towns and villages of Palestine 2000 years ago. We've tried to imagine what it would have been like to have been there. We've tried to understand what the day-to-day ministry of Jesus was like, what his followers were like, what his enemies were like. We've tried to get in touch with the truly revolutionary nature of Jesus' message.

We've learned that Jesus Christ has both a human and a divine nature and that Jesus was sent by God the Father to teach us about God and God's kingdom. Jesus' life was a continual teaching about God's reign of perfect peace, love, and justice.

We've even learned something from the cross of Jesus. We've learned that no matter what suffering or joy comes into our lives, God seeks our total trust and obedience. Our own suffering can be associated with Jesus' suffering, in imitation of him. We've learned that the cross is a symbol of the love of the Father and the Son for humankind. We've also learned that God keeps his promises.

You came to this course with ideas about Jesus that you had been gathering from your earliest years. Hopefully, you've been able to gain some new insights about Jesus, what he said, what he did, and why he did it. Now it's time for you to put all those ideas together and ask yourself, "Who is Jesus really, for me, now? What part is Jesus going to play in the rest of my life?"

Take your time before you answer, because how you answer can affect who you are for the rest of your life.

Looking for Answers!

Check the correct reference.

Jesus asks Peter, "Who do you say that I am?" Peter's response is:

_____ a. Luke 9:18–20

_____ b. Matthew 6:1–4

_____ c. Mark 9:30–32

_____ d. John 7:40–44

Answer: _____

What I have learned about Jesus in this course:

_____

_____

_____

What I have learned about God because of what I have studied about Jesus:

_____

_____

_____

Who I now believe Jesus is:

_____

_____

_____

_____

Reflection

[Peter, James, and John went with Jesus] to a place called Gethsemane; and he said to his disciples, "Sit here while I pray." . . . And going a little farther, he threw himself on the ground and prayed that, if it were possible, the hour might pass from him. He said, "Abba, Father, for you all things are possible; remove this cup from me; yet, not what I want, but what you want." He came and found them sleeping; and he said to Peter, "Simon, are you asleep? Could you not keep awake one hour? Keep awake and pray that you may not come into the time of trial; the spirit is indeed willing, but the flesh is weak." (Mark 14:32, 35–38)

Briefly discuss ways that young people today can improve their relationship with Jesus.

 This week, I will improve my relationship with Jesus by: _____

_____

Jesus,

Help me be open to God's will in my life and help me always to trust that God's will is what's best for me.

Give me perseverance and strength in my faith.

Help me always be aware of the power, love, and goodness of God, as well as your daily presence in my life.

Amen.

But there are also many things that Jesus did; if every one of them were written down, I suppose that the world itself could not contain the books that would be written. (John 21:25)

Homework

To review what you have learned in this chapter, find the following words in the puzzle:

```
O  B  E  D  I  E  N  C  E  A  B  C  G  D  B  O  D  Y  E  S  F
G  M  H  N  R  E  P  P  U  S  S  E  N  I  L  O  H  R  L  I  T
J  O  K  O  L  R  N  A  M  O  R  M  I  N  A  R  R  E  S  T  R
O  T  P  I  H  F  Q  S  N  R  S  T  K  U  S  V  E  F  W  X  U
M  Y  S  T  E  R  Y  S  Y  S  E  Y  G  Z  P  P  A  F  B  E  T
O  C  D  C  R  U  C  I  F  I  X  E  O  F  H  C  H  U  R  C  H
D  G  H  E  O  G  O  O  D  N  A  I  L  J  E  W  I  S  H  I  I
G  J  L  R  D  U  K  N  L  M  M  N  G  N  M  G  O  P  G  O  D
N  N  L  R  B  U  R  Y  Q  E  P  R  A  Y  Y  O  N  S  R  J  S
I  A  I  U  T  I  U  G  R  V  L  M  T  W  X  V  S  A  Y  E  T
K  Z  W  S  S  Z  A  U  E  B  E  C  H  D  E  E  L  L  R  E
F  A  N  E  F  I  L  G  H  S  I  T  A  F  N  R  J  V  I  P  M
L  R  E  R  K  I  O  E  H  L  A  M  A  D  O  N  N  A  N  O  P
H  E  W  H  A  Y  V  T  P  E  Q  T  N  R  T  O  L  T  I  G  L
S  T  A  F  R  I  E  N  D  S  H  I  P  J  S  R  T  I  A  U  E
U  H  L  S  L  G  L  I  V  E  K  V  S  E  L  T  S  O  P  A  E
P  I  L  A  T  E  G  A  R  D  E  N  T  S  U  R  T  N  C  R  R
W  X  Y  Z  M  E  S  S  I  A  H  A  J  U  D  A  S  B  D  D  H
E  S  A  V  I  O  R  F  G  H  C  R  O  S  S  C  H  R  I  S  T
```

alive	failure	Jewish	pain	sleep
apostles	Father	Judas	passion	Son
arrest	free	kindness	Pilate	stone
blasphemy	friendship	king	plan	suffer
body	garden	kingdom	pray	Supper
bury	Gethsemane	law	rejoice	Temple
Christ	God	life	resurrection	three
Church	Golgatha	love	rise	tomb
crucifix	good	Messiah	Roman	trial
cross	governor	mystery	saint	trust
death	guards	nail	salvation	truth
Easter	Herod	Nazareth	Savior	will
evil	holiness	new	scourge	yes
example	Jesus	obedience	sin	

Your Catholic Heritage

Traditional Prayers

Sign of the Cross

In the name of the Father,
and of the Son,
and of the Holy Spirit.
Amen.

The Lord's Prayer

Our Father, who art in heaven,
hallowed be your name;
your kingdom come;
your will be done on earth
as it is in heaven.
Give us this day our daily bread;
and forgive us our trespasses
as we forgive those
who trespass against us;
and lead us not into temptation,
but deliver us from evil. Amen.

Hail Mary

Hail, Mary, full of grace,
the Lord is with you!
Blessed are you among women,
and blessed is the fruit of your womb, Jesus.
Holy Mary, Mother of God,
pray for us sinners,
now and at the hour of our death.
Amen.

Trinity Prayer

Glory to the Father,
and to the Son,
and to the Holy Spirit.
As it was in the beginning, is now,
and will be forever. Amen.

La Señal de la Cruz

Por la señal de la Santz Cruz,
de nuestros enemigos libranos,
Señor, Dios nuestro.
En el nombre del Padre
y del Hijo
y del Espíritu Santo. Amén.

El Padre Nuestro

Padre nuestro, que estás en el cielo,
santificado sea tu nombre,
Venga a nosotros tu reino;
hágase tu voluntad en la tierra
como en el cielo.
Danos hoy nuestro pan de cade día;
perdona nuestras ofensas,
como también nosotros perdonamos
a los que nos ofenden,
No nos dejes caer en tentación,
y líbranos del mal. Amén.

El Ave María

Dios te salve, María, llena eres de gracia,
el Señor es contigo.
Bendita tú eres entre todas las mujeres,
y bendito es el fruto de tu vientre, Jesús.
Santa María, Madre de Dios,
ruega por nosotros pecadores,
ahora, y en la hora de nuestra muerte.
Amén.

La Oración a La Trinidad

Gloria al Padre, al Hijo, y al Espíritu Santo;
como era en el principio, ahora, y siempre,
por los siglos de los siglos. Amén.

Other Prayers

Blessing Before Meals

Bless us, O Lord, and these your gifts
which we are about to receive from your
goodness, through Christ our Lord. Amen.

Thanksgiving After Meals

We give you thanks for all your gifts, Almighty
God, living and reigning now and forever.
Amen.

Act of Contrition

O my God, I am sorry for my sins.
In choosing to sin and failing to do good,
I have sinned against you
and your Church.
I firmly intend, with the help of your Son,
to do penance and to sin no more. Amen.

Prayer to the Holy Spirit

Come, Holy Spirit, fill the hearts of your
   faithful,
And kindle in them the fire of your love.
Send forth your Spirit and they shall be
   created.
And you shall renew the face of the
   earth.
Lord, by the light of the Holy Spirit
you have taught the hearts of your faithful.
In the same Spirit
help us relish what is right
and always rejoice in your consolation.
We ask this through Christ our Lord. Amen.

Prayer of St. Alphonsus Liguori

Grant me the gift of knowledge, so I may
know the things of God and, enlightened by
your holy teaching, may walk without
deviation in the path of eternal salvation.

Serenity Prayer

O God, grant me the serenity
to accept the things I cannot change,
the courage to change the things I can,
and the wisdom to know the difference.
Amen.

The Jesus Prayer

Lord Jesus Christ,
Son of God,
have mercy on me, a sinner.
Amen.

Rules Catholics Live By

The Great Commandments

"Love the Lord your God
with all your heart
with all your soul
with all your strength, and
with all your mind;
love your neighbor as you love yourself."
(Luke 10:27; Deuteronomy 6:5; Leviticus 19:18)

Jesus' Law of Love

"Love one another as I have loved you." (John 15:12)

The Ten Commandments

1. I am the LORD your God. You shall not have strange gods before me.

2. You shall not take the name of the LORD your God in vain.

3. Remember to keep holy the LORD's day.

4. Honor your father and your mother.

5. You shall not kill.

6. You shall not commit adultery.

7. You shall not steal.

8. You shall not bear false witness against your neighbor.

9. You shall not covet your neighbor's wife.

10. You shall not covet your neighbor's goods.

Laws of the Church

1. You shall attend Mass on Sundays and on holy days of obligation and rest from servile work.

2. You shall confess your sins at least once a year.

3. You shall receive the Sacrament of the Eucharist at least during the Easter Season.

4. You shall observe the days of fasting and abstinence established by the Church.

5. You shall help provide for the needs of the Church.

Nicene Creed

We believe in one God,
the Father, the Almighty,
maker of heaven and earth,
of all that is seen and unseen.
We believe in one Lord, Jesus Christ,
the only Son of God,
eternally begotten of the Father,
God from God, Light from Light,
true God from true God,
begotten, not made, one in Being with the
  Father.
Through him all things were made.
For us men and for our salvation
he came down from heaven:
by the power of the Holy Spirit
he was born of the Virgin Mary, and became
  man.
For our sake he was crucified under Pontius
  Pilate;
he suffered, died, and was buried.

On the third day he rose again
in fulfillment of the Scriptures;
he ascended into heaven
and is seated at the right hand of the Father.
He will come again in glory
to judge the living and the dead,
and his kingdom will have no end.
We believe in the Holy Spirit, the Lord, the
  giver of life,
who proceeds from the Father and the Son.
With the Father and the Son he is
  worshiped and glorified.
He has spoken through the prophets.
We believe in one holy catholic and
  apostolic Church.
We acknowledge one baptism for the
  forgiveness of sins.
We look for the resurrection of the dead,
and the life of the world to come. Amen.

Eucharistic Prayer IV

Father, we acknowledge your greatness:

all your actions show your wisdom and love.

You formed man in your own likeness

and set him over the whole world

to serve you, his creator,

and to rule over all creatures.

Even when he disobeyed you and lost your friendship,

you did not abandon him to the power of death,

but helped all men to seek and find you.

Again and again you offered a covenant to man,

and through the prophets taught him to hope for salvation.

Father, you so loved the world

that in the fullness of time you sent

your only Son to be our Savior.

He was conceived through the power of the Holy Spirit,

and born of the Virgin Mary,

a man like us in all things but sin.

To the poor he proclaimed the good news of salvation,

to prisoners, freedom,

and to those in sorrow, joy.

In fulfillment of your will

he gave himself up to death;

but by rising from the dead,

he destroyed death and restored life.

And that we might live no longer for ourselves but for him,

he sent the Holy Spirit from you, Father,

as his first gift to those who believe,

to complete his work on earth

and bring us the fullness of grace.

Father, may this Holy Spirit sanctify these offerings.

Let them become the body and blood of Jesus Christ our Lord

as we celebrate the great mystery

which he left us as an everlasting covenant.

He always loved those who were his own in the world.

When the time came for him to be glorified by you, his heavenly Father,

he showed the depth of his love.

While they were at supper,

he took bread, said the blessing, broke the bread,

and gave it to his disciples, saying:

Take this, all of you, and eat it:

this is my body which will be given up for you.

In the same way, he took the cup, filled with wine.

He gave you thanks, and giving the cup to his disciples, said:

Take this all of you and drink from it:

this is the cup of my blood,

the blood of the new and everlasting covenant.

It will be shed for you and for all

so that sins may be forgiven.

Do this in memory of me.

Let us proclaim the mystery of faith:

A Christ has died,

   Christ is risen,

   Christ will come again.

B Dying you destroyed our death

   rising you restored our life.

   Lord Jesus, come in glory.

C When we eat this bread and drink this cup,

   we proclaim your death, Lord Jesus,

   until you come in glory.

D Lord, by your cross and resurrection

   you have set us free.

   You are the Savior of the world.

Father, we now celebrate this memorial of our redemption.

We recall Christ's death, his descent among the dead,

his resurrection and ascension to your right hand;

and, looking forward to his coming in glory,

we offer you his body and blood,

the acceptable sacrifice

which brings salvation to the whole world.

Lord, look upon this sacrifice which you have given to your Church;

and by your Holy Spirit, gather all who share this one bread and one cup

into the one body of Christ, a living sacrifice of praise.

Lord, remember those for whom we offer this sacrifice,

especially N. our Pope,

N. our bishop, and bishops and clergy everywhere.

Remember those who take part in this offering,

those here present and all your people,

and all who seek you with a sincere heart.

Remember those who have died in the peace of Christ

and all the dead whose faith is known to you alone.

Father, in your mercy grant also to us, your children,

to enter into our heavenly inheritance

in the company of the Virgin Mary, the Mother of God,

and your apostles and saints.

Then, in your kingdom, freed from the corruption of sin and death,

we shall sing your glory with every creature through Christ our Lord,

through whom you give us everything that is good.

Through him,

with him,

in him,

in the unity of the Holy Spirit,

all glory and honor is yours,

Almighty Father,

forever and ever.

Amen.

Catholic Devotions and Practices

The Rosary

The Joyful Mysteries

(Mondays and Thursdays)

1. The annunciation
2. The visitation
3. The birth of Jesus
4. The presentation in the Temple
5. Mary and Joseph find Jesus in the Temple

The Sorrowful Mysteries

(Tuesdays and Fridays)

1. The agony in the garden
2. The scourging of Jesus
3. The crowning with thorns
4. Jesus carries his cross
5. Jesus dies on the cross

The Glorious Mysteries

(Sundays, Wednesdays, and Saturdays)

1. The resurrection
2. The ascension
3. The Holy Spirit is sent upon the apostles
4. The assumption of Mary
5. Mary is crowned queen of heaven and earth

Stations of the Cross

First Station: Jesus is condemned to death.

Second Station: Jesus is made to carry his cross.

Third Station: Jesus falls for the first time.

Fourth Station: Jesus meets Mary, his mother.

Fifth Station: Simon, the Cyrenian, helps Jesus carry his cross.

Sixth Station: Veronica wipes the face of Jesus.

Seventh Station: Jesus falls the second time.

Eighth Station: Jesus speaks to the women of Jerusalem.

Ninth Station: Jesus falls the third time.

Tenth Station: Jesus is stripped of his clothing.

Eleventh Station: Jesus is nailed to the cross.

Twelfth Station: Jesus dies on the cross.

Thirteenth Station: Jesus is taken down from the cross.

Fourteenth Station: Jesus is laid in the tomb.

Prayer for the Way of the Cross

We adore you, O Christ, and we bless you,

because by your holy cross

you have redeemed the world.

Holy Days in the United States

Christmas, the Birth of Jesus—December 25

Solemnity of Mary, Mother of God—January 1

Ascension of the Lord—the fortieth day (Thursday) after Easter

Assumption of Mary into Heaven—August 15

All Saints' Day—November 1

Immaculate Conception of Mary—December 8

Days of Abstinence

(Days when Catholics age 14 and over do not eat meat)

Ash Wednesday

Fridays in Lent

Good Friday

Days of Fasting

(Days when Catholics ages 18–59 eat one full meal and two smaller meals)

Ash Wednesday

Good Friday

The Sacraments

Sacraments of Initiation

Baptism

Confirmation

Eucharist

Sacraments of Healing

Reconciliation

Anointing of the Sick

Sacraments of Vocation and Service

Matrimony

Holy Orders